THE ANARCHIST'S WORKBENCH

THE ANARCHIST'S WORKBENCH
By Christopher Schwarz

First published by Lost Art Press LLC in 2020
837 Willard St., Covington, KY 41011, USA
Web: http://lostartpress.com

Title: The Anarchist's Workbench
Author: Christopher Schwarz
Editor: Megan Fitzpatrick
Copy editor: Kara Gebhart Uhl
Distribution: John Hoffman

Third printing

Copyright information: This book is covered by a Creative Commons License, Attribution-NonCommercial 4.0 International (CC BY-NC 4.0). You are free to share, copy and redistribute the material in any medium or format. And to adapt — remix, transform and build upon the material. Under the following terms: Attribution — You must give appropriate credit, provide a link to the license, and indicate if changes were made. You may do so in any reasonable manner, but not in any way that suggests the licensor endorses you or your use. NonCommercial — You may not use the material for commercial purposes. Complete details on this license are at creativecommons.org.

ISBN: 978-1-7333916-5-8

This book was printed and bound in the United States.
Signature Book Printing, Inc.
8041 Cessna Ave.
Gaithersburg, MD 20879
http://signature-book.com

TABLE OF CONTENTS

Preface vii
1. Planting the Flag..1
2. Internal Doubt & Defiant Retort 6
3. For the Love of Yellow Wood 16
4. All the Mistakes...32
5. Before A.J. Roubo 82
6. Joinery, Like a Vow 98
7. Make it Damn Big (Mostly) 118
8. Workholding: Edges & Ends...............................132
9. Workholding: Faces of Boards 156
10. Afraid of Fire 176
11. Introduction to the Anarchist's Workbench 188
    Construction Drawings & Cutting List 206
12. Build the Benchtop 212
13. Build the Base 226
14. Assembly & Vises... 244
15. Make it Work Right 274
16. The 'A' is Now at the End 284

Appendices
A. Workbenches CAQ 290
B. Working Without a Workbench.........................302
C. Helpful Tools for Bench Builders 310
D. A Workbench Timeline 316

DUCTILE IRON HOLDFAST, AFTER A FRENCH EXAMPLE
One of the most effective workbench clamps is the traditional holdfast. Historically made from wrought iron, modern examples are steel or ductile iron.

PREFACE

At first glance, the workbench in this book appears to be almost identical to the bench I built in 2005, which has shown up in a number of magazines and books. It's chunky, made from yellow pine and the workholding is a leg vise, planing stop and holdfasts.

Despite their similarities, the workbench plan in this book is a significant improvement. During the last 15 years I have found better ways to laminate the top using fewer clamps, easier ways to make the massive joints, plus layout tricks here and there that result in tighter joints all around. The top is thicker, heavier and creates less waste when using 2x12 dimensional lumber.

The workholding is far more effective. Thanks to improvements in vise manufacturing and a mature understanding of how these vises work, the leg vise is strong enough to hold boards without the help of a sliding deadman. There is no parallel guide, so you can work at the vise without stooping. The planing stop uses a metal tooth, made by a blacksmith, that holds your work with a lot less sliding. And the pattern of holdfast holes in the top – something that took me years to get right – ensures there will almost always be a hole right where you need one.

The fact that the bench is similar to my bench from 2005 is somewhat of a comfort to me. It means I wasn't too far off the mark when I began my journey. And equally remarkable is that 15 years of building workbenches of all different forms, from Roman benches to a miniature one from Denmark, wasn't able to shake my conviction that a simple timber-framed bench is ideal for many woodworkers.

In addition to the fully matured workbench design, this book also dives a little deeper into the past to explore the origins of this form. I first encountered this type of bench in a French book from about 1774, and at the time I couldn't find much else written about it. Since then, libraries and museums have digitized their collections and opened them to the public. So we've been able to trace its origins back another 200 years and found evidence it emerged somewhere in the Low Countries or northern France in the 1500s. We also have little doubt there are more discoveries to be made.

And finally, the story of this bench is deeply intertwined with my own story as a woodworker, researcher, publisher and – of course – aesthetic anarchist.

That's why I've decided to give away the content of this book to the world at large. The electronic version of the book is free to download, reproduce and give away to friends. You can excerpt chapters for your woodworking club. Print it all out, bind it and give it away as a gift. The only thing you cannot do is sell it or make money off of it in any way. Put simply: Commercial use of this material is strictly prohibited. But other than that, go nuts.

If you prefer a nicely bound book instead of an electronic copy, we sympathize. That's what we prefer, too. So we are printing some copies of this book for people who prefer it in that format. Those will cost a bit of money to make (we don't make low-quality crap here at Lost Art Press) so we won't be able to give those away. But we will sell them – as always – at a fair price for a book that is printed in the United States, sewn, bound in fiber tape and covered in a durable hardback.

This book is the final chapter in the "anarchist" series – "The Anarchist's Tool Chest," "The Anarchist's Design Book" and now "The Anarchist's Workbench." And it is (I hope) my last book on workbenches. So it seemed fitting that to thank all the woodworkers who have supported me during this journey, this book should belong to everyone.

Christopher Schwarz
June 2020
Covington, Kentucky

PREFACE

ANTIQUE VISE SCREWS
BLACKSMITH-MADE VISE SCREWS, PROBABLY FRENCH, FOR SALE IN A STREET FAIR IN EUROPE.

COVINGTON WORKSHOP, 2016
OUR WORKSHOP WAS BUILT IN THE 19TH CENTURY AS A GERMAN BAR AND GROCERY, AND WAS A BAR OR CAFE UNTIL WE PURCHASED IT IN 2015.

CHAPTER I
PLANTING THE FLAG

I dragged my workbench into the 1896 German barroom and dropped it in front of the building's giant built-in cabinet – called the back bar – where the establishment's bottles of hard liquor were once arrayed in front of a 4' x 10' mirror.

God, I hate mirrors. But I turned to face it anyway.

Some days I wonder what brought me to that moment. I'd left a prestigious and well-paying job in publishing. A house in the suburbs. Four weeks of vacation. And I traded that for a worn-out bar in a red-light district in Covington, Ky. Why?

I think it had something to do with the death of my uncle.

That day I raised my phone and took a self-portrait: the bench, the mirror and me. This spot, right here at my workbench, is where I hope to die. That's where the story will end.

∧ ∧ ∧

This story begins when I was 28, insecure and (honestly) the worst woodworker I knew. My dad was a better craftsman. My uncle? Better. My best friend at the time? Definitely better. His wife? She was way better than all of us – a natural. But I had something that they didn't: a job at a woodworking magazine.

A national magazine. With 200,000 readers. A position that commands true respect.

Here's a snapshot of one of my earliest days, when a box arrived from California that was addressed to me.

"You don't f&*%ing deserve that," Jim spat. He eyed my new block plane with disgust. "You haven't earned it." With that, he walked away from my desk.

After shaking off the sucker punch, I decided Jim's outburst wasn't surprising. In his experience, every single thing in life had to be earned.

The *Popular Woodworking* Team

David Thiel
Associate Editor
Specialties: Projects, new products and tools, tricks of the trade
(513) 531-2690 ext. 255

Jim Stuard
Associate Editor
Specialties: Projects, carving, turning, project illustrations
(513) 531-2690 ext. 348

Christopher Schwarz
Managing Editor
Specialties: Article submissions, letters, reader contests
(513) 531-2690 ext. 407

STAFF BOX, *POPULAR WOODWORKING MAGAZINE*, 1997
MY FIRST PHOTO IN THE MAGAZINE. I AM BARELY OLD ENOUGH TO SHAVE.

Jim and I were both low-level editors at *Popular Woodworking Magazine* in about 1997. Like the other staff members (except me), Jim had come up through a series of commercial woodworking shops in Cincinnati, where the magazine was headquartered. At the time, there was little job security in the local shops. It was typical to be fired when the work slowed before Christmas then be rehired in the spring when the rich people wanted new kitchens. The pay sucked and the work was difficult, with most shops freezing cold in the winter and broiling in the summer.

So yeah, I could see how a young journalist (me) buying a $125 Lie-Nielsen block plane would piss Jim off.

During my lunch hour that day, I crept across the hall to the magazine's workshop and sharpened my new plane's iron at someone else's workbench. I was desperate to weasel my way into the magazine's workshop and earn a space to work. But to do that, I needed to stop borrowing their tools, which annoyed the piss out of them.

It had taken me months to save the money for the plane. My salary was $23,000 a year, which was pathetic even for the 1990s. After taxes and health insurance, I took home about $300 a week. My wife, Lucy, was also a low-paid journalist. And together we had a 1-year-old daughter, a mortgage and a shocking daycare bill. We would have been better off financially if I'd stayed at home.

But *Popular Woodworking* was a dream job. I was an enthusiastic and unremarkable home woodworker with a couple journalism degrees and six years of experience at newspapers and magazines. I took the job at *Popular Woodworking* because I was tired of getting shot at, screamed at and questioned by the state police (all part of a day's work in newspapers). A woodworking magazine seemed an ideal idyll.

When I landed the job at *Popular Woodworking*, my dad congratulated me (even though he unsecretly wanted me to be a lawyer).

"You're going to love being surrounded by carpenters," he said. "Salt of the earth people."

He got the salty part right.

With the block plane in hand, I thought I had enough tools to do some serious woodworking. I wanted to get back into dovetailing (which I had learned during night classes at the University of Kentucky). But I didn't have a workbench in the magazine's workshop. So, during lunch I'd step into the shop and work at someone else's bench and dispose of the evidence by the end of the hour. I was tolerated but not encouraged. My job description was to edit the words, work with the graphic designers, schedule photographers and meet the magazine's deadlines.

For me, that work took about 20 to 30 hours a week. And my desire to work in the shop was so strong it bordered on physical pain. So, I asked my boss, Steve, if I could have a bench in the shop. The answer: There are no open benches. Could I build a bench? Answer: "It's not your turn."

Like all woodworking magazines, we received regular shipments of free tools – crap we didn't even ask for. The tool manufacturers were gambling that we'd fall in love with their gizmos and write a tool review, producing almost-free publicity for them. One random box we received contained four brackets – I can't remember if they were plastic or aluminum. But they were designed to be a fast way to make sawhorses. You cut some pine 2x4s to size and screwed them into the brackets. Voilà – you had pair of sawhorses without cutting anything other than 90° and without having to muddle in any joinery.

I decided the sawhorses could become the base of a workbench. I'd just make the legs 35" long instead of 24". For the benchtop, I scored a beautiful veneered Art Deco walnut door from our warehouse. The door had been part of a huge system of folding doors to our building's cafeteria, back when it was a Coca-Cola plant.

    I screwed the door to the sawhorses and scavenged a tiny Wilton vise for one end. I drilled some dog holes. Done.

    After only one day of work, I had a bench. While no one was looking, I scooted aside the table for the shop's dry grinder and pushed my bench into place.

    And after only two days of work, I had a bench that I hated. It scooted, jittered or slid every time I sawed, planed or chiseled on it. When I finished planing a board, I had to drag the bench 3' back to the starting line to plane another board.

    Strangely, no one threw me or my bench into the dumpster. Jim scowled, but he held his tongue. I had planted my flag in the workshop. I was in.

    And so, at our next editorial planning meeting for the magazine I asked: Can I build a workbench?

    Steve: "It's not your turn."

PLANTING THE FLAG

BACK BAR, 837 WILLARD ST., 2016

AFTER STRIPPING THE BENCH ROOM DOWN TO THE STUDS WE FOUND EVIDENCE THAT THE FLOORBOARDS HAD BEEN LAID AT AN ANGLE ORIGINALLY. SO WE BUILT THE NEW FLOOR WITH THE SAME PATTERN.

A LOAD OF YELLOW PINE, LOWE'S, 2020
I PREFER TO BUY MY LUMBER FROM MOM-AND-POP LUMBERYARDS, SUCH AS HUBER LUMBER IN NORWOOD, OHIO. SOMETIMES, HOWEVER, THE HOME CENTER IS THE ONLY PLACE THAT HAS ENOUGH CLEAR STOCK.

CHAPTER II
INTERNAL DOUBT & DEFIANT RETORT

In the 1990s when I was desperate for a decent (or really, any) workbench, I wasn't alone.

Most serious hand-tool woodworkers I knew at the time owned some sort of European cabinetmaker's workbench. You know the type – sled feet, face vise, tail vise and a series of square dogs. There is a tool tray at the back. Below the benchtop might be a cabinet for storing tools and bench appliances. It's a good bench design (I own one), but it is a complex bench to build, and it is expensive to buy a good one.

As a result, most hobbyists I knew at the time had either a bench that was built into their shed or garage, or they had something more like my door-on-sawhorses bench – a makeshift worksurface that was fine for routing, sanding and other power-tool tasks. I also knew a lot of people who used old wooden desks (Hi, Keith!). Or a pile of cheap kitchen cabinets topped with a couple layers of plywood.

One of the problems we all faced in the 1990s was the lack of great workbench hardware in the catalogs. Jorgensen and Record still made decent quick-release vises, but if you wanted other varieties of new vises, your choices were limited. There were some no-name vise screws from Europe for making their native benches. Some horrible aluminum planing stops. And commercial holdfasts made from grey iron. They didn't hold your work until you struck them really hard. And if you hit them really hard, they would break (grey iron is a dumb material for holdfasts).

Oh, there was one really good workbench book, "The Workbench Book" (Taunton) by Scott Landis.

Since that time, the world of workbenches has changed for the better. There are companies both large and small that make quality commercial benches. There's so much vise hardware out there that people don't ask: Where can a I find a wooden screw for a leg vise? They ask: Who makes the best? Blacksmiths and large companies now make holdfasts and quality planing stops that are readily available to anyone

BENCHCRAFTED VISE COMPONENTS, GALENA, ILL., 2017
BUYING THE RAW MATERIALS FOR YOUR WORKBENCH FROM SMALL BUSINESSES SUPPORTS OTHER SMALL BUSINESSES, SUCH AS THE LEMFCO INC. FOUNDRY.

INTERNAL DOUBT & DEFIANT RETORT

with a computer.

Now the problem is different: There are almost too many bits of hardware to choose from. And too many words written about workbenches.

Perhaps this is like fighting high cholesterol with a package of cheese curds, but that's why this book exists. Say you don't want to read the 10 million workbench posts out there. Or sort through the 18.5 million videos (that was an April 2020 search) about building a workbench. Or ponder the thousands of iterations possible for the following simple equation: style of bench, plus type of face vise, plus type of tail vise.

How about one short book? One that wraps it all up?

Could that book discuss all the workbenches I have built but really distill the designs down to one bench – the conclusion of decades of cycles of research, construction and use? And could the book (and that one bench) reflect the way I live as an American aesthetic anarchist?

That last sentence might have made you wince. Why discuss a fringe philosophy in a book about a chunky table with vises? If you haven't thought much about the act of making things, that's OK. But let me assure you that building durable objects these days is a radical deal.

So here's a brief (I promise) explanation. I'm not out to convert anybody to anything. But I do want to explain the title of the book.

American aesthetic anarchism is often confused with nihilism or rampant lawlessness. In truth, anarchism – and its underlying idea of "mutualism" – has little to do with violence or overthrowing the government. Please look them up if you don't believe me. Most American anarchists (like most Democrats and Republicans) are peace-loving, justice-seeking normal people.

Anarchists think the scales of justice have probably never worked properly. The big companies, the governments and the churches happen to own the scales. And they know how to make them work in their favor.

You've probably noticed that giant corporations are the single most powerful force in our economy – far more important than individuals or small businesses. Economic growth and expansion is their goal, year over year over year. As a result, our economy is driven by endless consumerism. Another by-product: Products that were once durable (such as furniture) are now disposable (hey, I know you know this). And so we spend money to replace things that once lasted a lifetime – things such as a simple dining room set or bookshelves (ya, we can't even make bookshelves right).

You don't have to live like this. You can trade your handmade furniture for a pair of home-sewn pants, or get your eggs from the people who also feed the chickens. Don't buy from Amazon or S-Mart if you can avoid it (truth: sometimes I cannot avoid it). In most towns there's a baker, a butcher and candlestick maker who have somehow survived economic apocalypse. You can shop there.

Or take the bigger step. Quit your corporate job and join the ranks of the candlestick makers. Build things that can be repaired and will never need replacing. Tip the scales of commerce the other way with your dirty thumb.

You don't even have to call this anarchism. You can call it pre-capitalism. The barter system. Or just being neighborly.

So, getting back to the question, how could a workbench design reflect my ideas about a more pleasant and just society? You can skip ahead to Chapter 11 if you want to see where I ended up. Or you can follow the bright string I've rolled out for you through these early chapters as I build the argument for this bench design. If you follow the string, you might end up with a different ideal design, even if we embrace the same criteria for what makes a good bench. And that's OK, neighbor.

Here, however, is where I begin:

• A workbench should never have to be replaced or upgraded. I'm not a fan of tools, furniture or anything that becomes obsolete. Mass-market workbenches, much like mass-market tools, have a short lifespan. That way you are obligated to buy another tool or workbench on down the line. This feeds a wasteful machine.

• The workbench should be made using raw materials and components from small businesses or individuals whenever possible. By and large this stuff is better. And purchasing it (or bartering for it) helps support individual makers and business owners, just like you. That relationship – individuals helping individuals – has always made sense to me. Another great alternative is to get your wood from places that recycle construction waste. I've built benches with the leftover logs from a timber frame site – their offcuts are easily big enough to make a bench.

• The workbench should help you make furniture that never needs replacing. In many ways, the workbench is the mother of all my thoughts about furniture and society. With your bench and your tools, you can make furniture for customers and loved ones that ends the stupid cycle of 1) buy a bookcase, 2) use it until it falls apart, 3) buy another bookcase.

Oh, I had one more question. Could this book not be the "Indiana Jones and the Kingdom of the Crystal Skull" of my career?

Let's find out.

Where to begin? Let's start with the most common question I get from would-be workbench builders: What species of wood is best for making a bench?

The answer to that question also happens to be the most important lesson I learned when I built my first "real" workbench. Here it is: Yellow pine (and construction lumber in general) is the bench-builder's friend.

∧ ∧ ∧

After struggling with my door-on-sawhorses workbench, I found myself sneaking back for a conjugal visit with the other benches in the magazine's workshop. Most of the other benches consisted of thin benchtops (which had been massive doors in a previous life) perched on top of kitchen-cabinet-like bases with drawers and doors. They all had quick-release vises, but that was about all they offered for workholding.

Jim's turn to build a workbench had come, and he had a newly built workbench with a massive patternmaker's vise and a tail vise with a system of dogs. But its biggest advantage was its thick top, which you could easily clamp stuff to. Jim had chosen hard maple for the benchtop because it was difficult to purchase steamed European beech locally. And hard maple is similar in weight and stiffness to beech. (If you want to see it, search "Bullet-proof Bench" at *Popular Woodworking*.)

Small magazines run on a shoestring, and the maple had cost us a (relative) fortune – $800. I knew that fact because I'd approved the

HILL TOP LANE HOUSE, ARKANSAS
The second house we built outside Hackett, Ark. Much of the house was built with yellow pine. The wing under construction was the bedrooms for me and my three sisters.

invoice and had to manage the workshop's annual budget. I knew there was no way I'd amass that kind of money for wood on my own – it was more than my monthly mortgage. Plus, it was unlikely that the magazine would ever shell out that kind of money for my workbench. I was just a word-herder.

One weekend day I was at our local home center to buy a paintbrush, spackle or who the hell knows. As I walked by the lumber section, I was stopped short by a sharp and familiar smell. Someone was cutting yellow pine on the store's radial-arm saw and hit a pungent sap pocket. It smelled like scorched turpentine, and suddenly I was 11 years old again in Hackett, Arkansas.

Yes, it's time for a flashback, the mark of quality literature.

My parents were hippie-adjacent, back-to-the-land people. Soon after moving to Arkansas when I was 5, they bought an 84-acre farm in the Boston Mountains and made plans to build our house there.

INTERNAL DOUBT & DEFIANT RETORT

My parents took a homebuilding class at the Shelter Institute in Bath, Maine, and suddenly every weekend we were camped out in a dark and buggy Arkansas forest. No electricity. No running water.

The two things I remember most: the wool blanket of humidity stuffed down my throat and the smell of yellow pine.

In the South and most of the Midwest, yellow pine is the preferred construction material for the frames of houses – joists, rafters, plates and headers. Some stud walls can be made from weaker stuff, but yellow pine is a must for the load-bearing components.

I knew from years of helping my dad build our houses that yellow pine was dense and strong. And when you found a board that was full of sap, it felt like you were hauling a steel beam instead of a wooden 2x12. And its smell – equally strong.

At the home center, with the sap in my nostrils, I walked to the ceiling-high racks of yellow pine, enough for 10 workbenches right there. I crouched down to look at the price tag for a 12'-long 2x8. It was $9.57.

If yellow pine was strong enough to build a house, would it be strong enough to build a workbench? Without any facts whatsoever, I decided that it was. And the next week I talked to my boss.

"What if I could build a fully functioning workbench for less than $200?" I asked Steve. "Could we print that story? We could call it: The $175 Workbench."

Steve looked skeptical, but I had a construction drawing, a cutting list and – most important – a price list of everything I needed, down to the last fender washer.

One of the things you must know about editing a magazine is that there's nothing so appealing to an editor as a gimmick or a good coverline. There was a legend in our company that the editor of *Men's Health* once came up with a genius coverline while he was on an airplane. It was so juicy that as soon as the plane landed, he called up the magazine and told them to commission a writer to create a story to match the coverline.

The coverline? "Bed-Busting Sex."

I totally believe that story is true.

Steve, however, was unsure about using yellow pine for a workbench.

THE ANARCHIST'S WORKBENCH

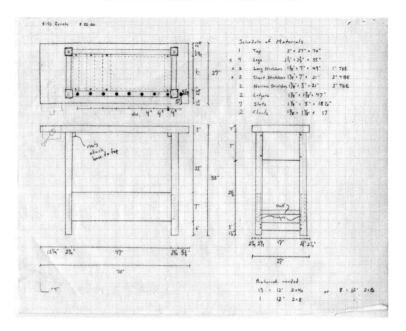

CONSTRUCTION DRAWING, $175 WORKBENCH, 2000
THE DRAWING I PRESENTED TO STEVE SHANESY TO GET PERMISSION TO BUILD THE $175 WORKBENCH (IT IS LABELED THE $150 WORKBENCH, BUT THE MATH DIDN'T WORK).

"If it's strong enough to build a house, it's got to be strong enough for a workbench," I said, turning my internal doubt into a defiant retort.

Steve looked at my drawing. He asked a few questions then tilted his head, like he was in for a long think.

Then I blurted: "I'll pay for all the wood. It won't cost the magazine a thing."

Steve: "Sold."

Now I had to find out if my boast about yellow pine was right. It was time to hit the books – and the lumberyard.

YELLOW PINE, HOT SPRINGS, ARK.
AFTER YEARS OF WORKING WITH YELLOW PINE ON OUR ARKANSAS FARM, I CONVINCED MYSELF IT WAS AN IDEAL WOOD FOR A WORKBENCH.

CHAPTER III
FOR THE LOVE OF YELLOW WOOD

This following chapter should be the shortest one in the book and should consist of only the following paragraph.

The wood for your workbench should be the heaviest and cheapest stuff that you can obtain with great ease. Let it dry a bit before you build your bench. When you mill it, discard any bits that twist a lot or split.

Sadly, I know that paragraph won't do because first-time bench-builders have enormous anxiety about every aspect of the project, especially the wood. And people who have built only one workbench (or watched a guy do it once) have fierce opinions on the topic that they spread far and wide.

The truth is that the number of wood species that are questionable for building a workbench is tiny. So, let's talk about those first. Here are the woods I would avoid, if possible.

WHITE PINES

I've built benches with white pines and they are sub-optimal for a couple reasons: weight and hardness. They are strong enough; mostly I object to how lightweight they are. A good furniture maker's bench should be heavy so that it won't move or shake while you work. White pines are remarkably lightweight, which is a great characteristic when making a tool chest (which should be mobile). *[Editor's note: Dude. That's my bench you're dissing. I weighed it down. It's fine.]*

A typical cubic foot of Eastern white pine (*Pinus strobus*) weighs 25 lbs. at 12 percent moisture content. A typical cubic foot of hard maple (*Acer saccharum*) is 44 pounds. That's a big difference. Also, white pines dent when you look at them sideways. That's not a deal killer, but it's annoying.

Bottom line: I'll use white pines for some parts in a bench, such as the stretchers or shelf boards, when the rest of the bench is made from dense stuff. But an all-white-pine bench is not my first choice.

WHITE PINE WORKBENCH, 2010
MEGAN FITZPATRICK'S SECOND WORKBENCH WAS BUILT USING WHITE PINE OFFCUTS FROM A LOG HOME.

ESCHEW EXOTICS

The other extreme is to build your bench out of a wood with properties more like steel than cellulose. Purpleheart (*Peltogyne spp.*) is a prime example. A cubic foot of this atrocity weighs 56 lbs. at 12 percent moisture content. That weight seems ideal for the bench builder who wants mass. But working with it is agonizing. It brutalizes your tools, both hand and power. (Plus it looks like a Smurf with a skin disease.) Ipe (*Handroanthus spp.*) is another prime example. A cubic foot weighs a ridiculous 69 lbs. Cutting it with regular woodworking tools is like trying to gum a carrot to death.

Plus, these woods are stupid expensive compared to the woods easily available to a North American woodworker. If I lived in South America and could purchase these woods for a reasonable price, I'd probably give them some love. But here in the Northern Hemisphere, there are many cheaper woods that are plenty heavy and easier to work.

FOR THE LOVE OF YELLOW WOOD

CHERRY SLABS, COLUMBUS, OHIO, 2010
At first glance, the slabs seemed big enough and sound enough to make a workbench. But the rot caused some problems.

AVOID SPONGY WOODS

If a tree has been sitting on the ground a while, it's likely that decay has set in. And the bugs built this city on rot and mold. Some of these trees end up at your lumberyard, especially if the seller deals in live-edge slabs or big pieces of wood for fireplace mantles.

Semi-rotted wood is fine for a conference table or fireplace mantle. That's because it won't see much abuse (and it likely will see a lot of epoxy). But if you put that same wood in a workbench, disaster might find you.

One of my workbenches had a thick benchtop of black cherry (*Prunus serotina*) that had been sitting out in the parking lot of a woodworking shop for a couple seasons. The price ($0.00) was right, and I could see some areas of the top were spongy. So, I filled these voids with a flexible epoxy that I tinted black. This was in 2010, and – oh my lord I just realized that this fact puts me at the forefront of the "big

REPAIR TO A ROTTED SECTION
DESPITE THE EPOXY, A CHUNK OF THE BENCH HAD TO BE BOLTED BACK ON.

slabs with epoxy pour" movement. Kill me.

Anyway, the epoxy wasn't strong enough to stabilize the entire cherry slab for use as a benchtop. And during a public event a couple years later, Roy Underhill knocked a chunk off the benchtop while setting a holdfast in it. (And that's why there are now two giant lag screws in its front edge.)

So, check any slabs for punkiness before purchasing. Probe any discolored areas with a pocket-knife, which will plunge into the bits that are too soft. Here's one more clue: If you pick up a slab and it seems entirely too lightweight, it's probably been turned into a Golden Corral by the insect world. Put the slab back.

SOME RED HERRINGS

If you remove the above three kinds of woods from your list of potential species, you still have an enormous range from which to choose.

But some people will insist that you narrow it down even more. Don't let them. Some people just like to be a bossy-pants, and so they come up with other hurdles for you to leap over when choosing a wood. Here are some dumb pieces of advice trying to lead you astray.

Use only light-colored species. This advice seems to make sense at first. A lightly colored bench will reflect light in a dark shop. It also will be easy to sight your plane soles against the benchtop to determine if its cutter is centered in the mouth.

But in reality, its hue doesn't make a ding-dong bit of difference.

Light-colored benches become dark with age. Dark-colored benches become light with age. Everything ends up as middling brown. I've seen old maple benches that look like walnut. And old walnut benches that look like maple. And working on either of these benches is no problem whatsoever. If you are struggling, sight that plane sole against a piece of wood on your bench. Or the floor. Or a piece of paper.

I'd probably pass on building an ebony bench because it's just an expensively dumb choice for a workbench. But if I had some nice walnut or cherry that was dirt cheap and thick, I'd turn it into a bench without remorse.

Dumb advice, part two: Use only a closed-pore or diffuse-pore species. The theory here is that if you use an open-pored species, such as ash or oak, then the pores might collect metal filings or other debris that will scratch your work. I have never, ever found this to be a problem. Oak, ash and other open-pore species are great for building workbenches.

Part three: Use only hardwood for your benchtop. Again, this seems to make sense on the surface. A hard benchtop is nice. But "hardwoods" aren't always hard. Basswood (*Tilia americana*) is an American hardwood. But it's as easily dented as Eastern white pine. If a hard benchtop is your goal, then you need to start comparing the different Janka ratings of the species on your short list.

Janka hardness is a number that expresses the pounds of force required to push a steel ball (that is .444" in diameter) halfway into a board. It's a number you can easily look up if you want to go down the Janka rabbit hole.

I tend to lurk around the rim of the Janka rabbit hole. If the wood is really soft (Eastern white pine's Janka rating is 380 pounds-force) I want to know that before I get building. (By way of comparison, hard maple's Janka rating is 1,450 pounds-force. Ipe's is a ridiculous 3,510 pounds-force.) The hardness of a species is something to consider, but it's not my first concern. So, what is?

How much the wood costs, per pound.

That might sound weird. Let's talk about it.

LET'S TALK ABOUT WEIGHT

When you compare the weights of species, you need to make sure the comparisons are all at the same moisture content (12 percent is the typical comparison unit). You can compare the density of a species by comparing its "specific gravity," which is a method that compares the weight to a cubic meter of water. Or you can look at the average dried weight of a cubic foot of the wood (also at 12 percent moisture content).

These are useful, but I think you can also make some important comparisons by factoring in the local price of a species. It's like buying meat at the butcher. Is rib eye ritzier than hamburger? The price per pound helps us answer that question (and yes, it is).

For example, a cubic foot of hard maple consists of 12 board feet of maple. If maple is $4.73 a board foot, then a cubic foot of maple costs $56.76. That cubic foot weighs 44 lbs. Or $1.29/pound.

Longleaf pine (a yellow pine) is 78 cents a board foot (for No. 1 grade), so a cubic foot costs $9.40. That cubic foot weighs 41 lbs. Or a remarkably cheap 23 cents per pound.

Because I live to poke fun at Ipe, let's run those numbers. Ipe costs $17 a board foot, so a cubic foot costs $204. That cubic foot weighs 69 lbs. So Ipe is $2.96/pound. Not a great deal at the wood butcher's.

The chart at right compares some of the common U.S. hardwoods and softwoods using typical Midwestern retail prices circa 2020 (this is not wholesale or trade pricing). This cost-per-pound calculation is simple to do yourself using your local prices.

Here's how: Take your cost per board foot (use 8/4 prices) and multiply that by 12. That's the cost for a cubic foot. Now divide that number by the weight of a cubic foot of that species (a statistic that is easily found in books and online). The result is the cost per pound.

Woods by the Pound*

Species	Cost (bf)	Weight (cubic ft.)	Cost per cubic ft.	Cost (per pound)
Cypress	$4.25	32	$51.00	$1.59
Douglas fir**	$1.24	32	$14.84	$0.46
Eastern White Pine	$1.90	25	$22.80	$0.91
Western Red Cedar	$3.25	23	$39.00	$1.70
Yellow pine**	$0.78	41	$9.40	$0.23
Alder (red)	$4.70	28	$56.40	$2.01
Ash	$3.92	42	$47.04	$1.12
Basswood	$3.12	26	$37.44	$1.44
Cherry	$6.95	35	$83.40	$2.38
Hard maple	$4.73	44	$56.76	$1.29
Hickory	$5.09	50	$61.08	$1.22
Ipe	$17.00	69	$204.00	$2.96
Poplar	$2.60	35	$31.20	$0.89
Red oak	$4.55	44	$54.60	$1.24
Soft maple	$3.87	38	$46.44	$1.22
Walnut	$10.55	38	$126.60	$3.33
White oak	$7.82	47	$93.84	$2.00
Yellow birch	$5.41	43	$64.92	$1.51

*Midwestern prices in 8/4 rough when possible.

**These were based on actual dimensions of a 2x12. A 2x12 is actually 1-1/2" x 11-1/4". So, a 2x12 x 8' contains 11-1/4 board feet of wood. If that 2x12 costs $8.81, then it is 78 cents per board foot. Or $9.40 for a cubic foot.

THE ANARCHIST'S WORKBENCH

YELLOW PINE NEEDLES, HOT SPRINGS, ARK.
Yellow pines are identified by how their needles are bundled on a twig. Yellow pines typically have two, three or five needles per fascicle (or bundle).

DO THE MATH

From the chart, ash looks like a good choice among the hardwoods. The problem with that assessment is that by the time you are reading this book, white ash might be almost extinct. The emerald ash borer has devastated the ash forests in the United States. So, you might not be able to buy it at any price. And if you do find it, you want to ensure it hasn't rotted. We have been plagued by punky ash for the last few years as the sawyers have milled up trees that have been standing dead.

Aside from ash, poplar and the maples are a great bang for the buck. Both are easy to work, readily available and fairly cheap by the pound. I've made workbenches using all three species and think they're fine. Neither is considered a noble species for a workbench, like European beech. But as long as you aren't out to impress anyone, go for it. You'll

FOR THE LOVE OF YELLOW WOOD

$175 WORKBENCH AFTER 20 YEARS OF USE, 2020

THE YELLOW PINE IN THIS WORKBENCH IS NOW ABOUT AS HARD AS MAPLE AND MOVES LITTLE WITH THE SEASONS.

have no problem finding those species at almost any lumberyard in America.

But if you want to go full redneck, read on.

Softwoods that are used for structural members in home construction – the yellow pines, Douglas fir, hemlock and some spruces – are an outstanding value. They are heavy, cheap and readily available at any lumberyard. After working with them most of my life in residential construction and workbench building, they remain my No. 1 choice for workbenches.

Here's why: Anyone can buy it. You don't have to search out a specialty lumberyard or set up a commercial account. Just go to the home center if you want (though I always prefer family lumberyards). They have plenty.

Also important: They have plenty. A typical home center or family lumberyard will have hundreds of planks of 2x material in the racks on any given day – everything from 2x6s to 2x12s – with lengths from 8' to 16'. At a home center, you can spend hours sifting through the racks to find the best boards – the employees don't care. At a family lumberyard it pays to ask permission (they will sometimes be happy to help you). Either way, just be sure to restack the lumber nicer than you found it.

Here's another buying tip: Some lumberyard chains carry No. 2 yellow pine, others carry No. 1. The price difference is minimal, but the quality isn't. No. 1 is worth the extra nickels. If you find a yard that deals in No. 1, you might be able to buy all the wood for your bench in one swoop. If you buy No. 2, you might have to hit all the yards in your town, county or region.

Yellow pine is easy to work. I've built yellow pine workbenches using only hand tools, and using a full-on machine shop. It's friendly stuff. Yes, there can be some knots, but if you pick your boards with care, you'll have almost none of those to deal with.

So there must be disadvantages. Yes, but they are slight. Construction lumber is sold in a wetter state than hardwood lumber. While hardwoods are typically sold at about 12 percent moisture content (or at equilibrium with some environment) that is not the case with construction lumber. It is wetter.

How wet? In the Midwest it might be 15-20 percent moisture content. On the West Coast, it might be even wetter (as in wet enough to ooze and squirt water). So, you need to gather up what you need to build your bench, cut it to rough length, stack it and wait a bit.

It might also be "case hardened" because it was kiln dried too quickly. When lumber is rushed through a kiln it can develop tension that is released when you cut it. It's particularly obvious when you rip a board. Sometimes the wood will pinch so hard on a blade it will stop a 3-horsepower table saw like pinching out a candle.

How do you deal with this? It's not difficult.

1. Plan to cut things a bit over-wide. And have some wooden wedges handy to keep the kerf open when you rip the wood. After that first rip, a case-hardened board will usually lose all of its fight.

2. Make your rip cut to a shallow depth at first – less than half the thickness of the board. Then raise the blade, flip the board end-over-end and finish the rip.

The final disadvantage: Softwoods are uber-redneck. No one is going to "ooh and ahh" over your choice of yellow pine. It's the mullet of the forest.

∧ ∧ ∧

THE TRUE COST OF YELLOW PINE PER POUND

I'm not a trusting soul. After I calculated the cost of yellow pine per pound (23 cents) based on published statistics, I decided to see if that worked in the real world. So, I weighed several 2x12x8s and came up with an average weight of 30.4 pounds each.

These were boards I'd had in my shop for months, so they had likely lost some of their water weight (as all softwoods do). Plus, the boards in this particular pile were fairly average – not full of sap or with lots of heavy summerwood. In other words, they were a bit on the light-weight side.

Each of these boards cost $8.81 each, so that's 29 cents per pound – about 6 cents per pound more expensive than the published weight tables indicate. But still a great deal.

I wondered, how did that work out after surfacing the boards and gluing them up? What was the cost per pound of "finished" yellow pine?

POPULAR WOODWORKING, FEBRUARY 2001
THE OPENING SPREAD FOR THE $175 WORKBENCH ARTICLE, MY FIRST PUBLISHED WORKBENCH PLAN.

Here's how I calculated that. The benchtop for the workbench at the end of this book is made from nine 2x12s, ripped in half, glued up and planed so the top is 5" thick. Nine 2x12 x 8s cost $79.29. After gluing up the top, I managed to weigh it on a heavy-duty scale we use for shipping crates. The top weighed 240 pounds. That's 33 cents per pound. Still a bargain (if you ask me).

BACK TO THE $175 WORKBENCH

As I built the "$175 Workbench" for *Popular Woodworking* I encountered all the advantages and disadvantages of yellow pine mentioned above. A fair number of the boards were case hardened, so getting them ripped and glued up was a challenge. It took two of us to wrangle the laminations for the benchtop.

But, and here's the kicker, I still own that workbench. And it has taught me other important lessons about construction-grade softwoods, yellow pine in particular. Here are two: It doesn't move much in service and it gets harder and harder with age.

True and embarrassing fact: When I started woodworking, I assumed that softwoods moved more with the seasons than hardwoods. This was based on working with home center softwoods. I'd buy what I needed and start working it the same day. By the end of the day, the wood would be a warped mess. And sometimes unusable.

The real problem was that the pine was wet and hadn't acclimated to my workshop. And – here's another fun fact – all woods tend to move a lot as they expunge that last little bit of water to become at balance with their environment.

So, I was working with pine at the worst possible time.

If you let softwoods dry for a few weeks, the stuff barely moves at all when you plane it and saw it. In general, softwoods move less in service than hardwoods.

I also love how yellow pine gets tougher with age. I'm told that this is because the sap hardens, first to copal then (after a couple million years) into amber. The difference is dramatic. When I purchase newly cut yellow pine, I can dent its soft earlywood with my knuckle or fingernail. After a year or two, it seems as hard as Formica.

My yellow pine bench was still soft and spongy when I finished it in 2000. Soon after that, the magazine had an evening event where we brought in a bunch of local readers. We did this sort of social event every few months or so. Sometimes it was for a focus group. Sometimes it was to test some new tools from a particular manufacturer. After this event, a bunch of readers gathered around my new workbench and asked questions, which went something like this: "Nice bench but, yellow pine?"

Once again, I was unprepared. All I could manage to say was that it was cheap and heavy. The readers didn't disagree with me, but they also weren't impressed.

That's when I decided to plow into the book "Wood Handbook: Wood as an Engineering Material," which is published by the U.S. Department of Agriculture. This book is free online – our tax dollars paid for it – and it is filled with all the numbers and terms that will impress people: modulus of elasticity, modulus of rupture, rolling shear strength, tensile strength and (the term that will always get you laid if you bring it up at a bar) Poisson's ratio. I also learned that most wooden roller coasters and telephone poles are made from yellow pine.

The "Wood Handbook" proved what I knew in my heart: yellow pine is an outstanding workbench material. It is heavy, strong and stiff. I then had the numbers, and I could use them to defend my choice of yellow pine.

However, there's no need to get into a discussion of those facts and figures. Or to reproduce the tables that explore wood as an engineering material. That's because any decent design for a workbench renders most of those tabular charts moot. If you make your benchtop so it's between 4" and 6" thick, even balsa wood is technically stiff enough to do the job. Pick a somewhat heavy species, and your thick benchtop will provide all the weight and stiffness you need – even if your bench's legs are white pine.

In other words, a thick benchtop renders the pointy-headed statistics a bit meaningless. Simply overbuild your bench – especially the benchtop – and almost any species will do.

FOR THE LOVE OF YELLOW WOOD

YELLOW PINE BARK, HOT SPRINGS, ARK.
THE BARK OF MOST YELLOW PINES RESEMBLES TECTONIC PLATES.

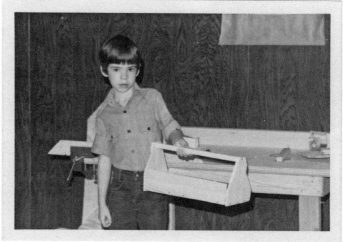

FORT SMITH, ARK., 1975

MY GRANDFATHER AND I BUILT THIS WORKBENCH IN OUR GARAGE (YES, WE HAD SWANKY PANELING) USING 1X4S AND PLYWOOD.

CHAPTER IV
ALL THE MISTAKES

Selecting the species of wood for a workbench is easy – almost any wood that is sound and fairly dry will do the job. Deciding how to put those sticks of wood together is where the real agony begins.

You could just pick a style of bench that looks good, or a design used by a woodworker you admire. You could buy a bench that is on sale. Those approaches can work. But they might not (and then you have to put your bench to sleep and bury it in the backyard).

After building the $175 Workbench, I had the time, energy and floorspace to investigate different workbench forms, build them and work on them. (I also worked for a magazine that was hungry for articles about building workbenches and shop equipment.) This chapter details most of those forms and how they have fared in a working shop.

But before we start comparing one bench design to another, it's a good time to think about what type of woodworker you are and what kind of woodworker you hope to be. Because that little bit of dime-store psychology can help you make some important decisions.

5 WORKBENCH FORMS

Different workbench forms are broadly allied with different woodworking trades. An obvious example is how the shaving horse (which is a low, staked workbench) is used for all manner of green woodworking tasks, from rural chairmaking to making rakes, drags and hoes. And while I'm sure that it's possible to build a Boulle-work cabinet on a shaving horse, it's not an ideal place for it.

So as you choose the form of workbench you want to build or buy, consider the tradition your work falls into. This will help you narrow your choices and perhaps avoid building three wrong benches before you get it right.

I think there are five common traditional forms for Western workbenches.

THE ANARCHIST'S WORKBENCH

CHESTER CORNETT'S WORKBENCH, MID-20TH CENTURY
Staked workbenches have been in use from Roman times (at the least) up to the present day. This bench, made from a section of a log, was used for chairmaking and other chores.

1. STAKED WORKBENCHES

The earliest form of workbench we know of is a long and narrow slab, usually about knee-high. It has three to eight legs, which are tenoned and wedged into the slab. Sometimes the tenons are round; sometimes they are square.

This early form bench shows up everywhere in Greek and Roman cultures (and the places they conquered). For many centuries there were both waist-high and knee-high versions of this bench form.

When looking at period paintings and drawings, this bench appears to have been used for a wide variety of tasks and trades. You find people handplaning on it. Building boats. General carpentry. Chairmaking.

The workholding could range from none – you used your body to secure the work – up to a fairly complex clamping mechanism that created what we now call the shaving horse.

Other common workholding devices include metal planing stops,

ALL THE MISTAKES

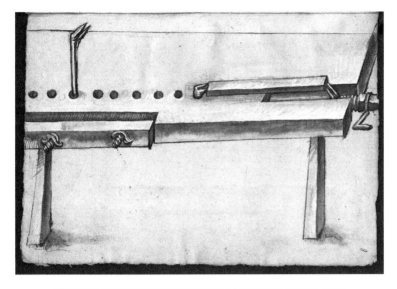

STAKED WORKBENCH WITH MODERN VISES, 1505
Staked workbenches were the dominant form until the 16th century. Shown is a staked workbench from Nürnberg, Germany.

holdfasts, notches, pegs and simple screw-driven vises. In some societies where this bench survived, it became quite specialized. I've seen variants in South America that are used for lutherie. And the low, staked bench was modified in Northern Europe for woodworkers who made buckets and casks, wheels and shingles. There are even extant low staked benches that have a modern tail vise and face vise.

But where this bench seems to excel is with most green woodworking tasks. Its low stance makes it ideal for using your body's weight as a clamp, plus hewing with a hatchet, crosscutting, mortising and planing. It's not as ideal for tasks that are more easily done while standing, such as cutting fancy dovetails.

The low staked bench also survived for many centuries among chairmakers who built post-and-rung chairs. Most importantly, it was a drilling station. The chair components could be secured with wedges and conveniently drilled with the woodworker standing over

EARLY TIMBER-FRAMED BENCH, C. 1580
IN THE 16TH CENTURY, WORKBENCHES WITH SQUARED JOINTS BEGAN TO APPEAR IN THE HISTORICAL RECORD.

ALL THE MISTAKES

TIMBER-FRAMED SHAKER WORKBENCH, OHIO
THE SIMPLE TIMBER-FRAMED BENCH DEVELOPED IN THE 16TH CENTURY WAS STILL A COMMON FORM IN THE 19TH CENTURY.

the work. In fact, these benches are still found in the hills of Appalachia and the Ozarks.

I built a few of these benches and, after using them for a few years, am convinced they are ideal for green woodworkers and those who pursue rural and farm woodcraft.

PROS: Simple construction requiring few tools. Usable for a wide variety of green woodworking tasks.
CONS: It can be challenging to hold work for fine joinery. Thick slab construction can result in the benchtop warping. Angled legs don't allow you to easily add a shelf.

2. TIMBER-FRAMED BENCHES

These workbenches are constructed like a timber-framed building. The components are big and squared off. The joints are square mortise-and-tenon joints, usually pegged, and arranged with lots of right angles (and sometimes a 45° angle or two). The top is typically a single slab of thick timber. These benches begin to show up in the written record in the 15th and 16th centuries, a prime example being Hieronymus Wierix's title page for the book "The Life of the Infant" (circa 1580).

This form of bench also shows up in Germany, England and France. While this form was made famous in the 18th century by A.J. Roubo's multi-volume "l'Art du menuisier," it would be a mistake to label all of these stout timber-framed benches as "Roubo workbenches."

This form of bench shows up everywhere, including in Shaker villages. The massive and famous workbench at Hancock Shaker Village in Massachusetts is essentially a timber-framed workbench with eight drawers and two doors. Recently I encountered another similar Shaker bench in one of the Western communities that was smaller and didn't have doors or drawers. This 19th-century bench looked like a copy of the bench from the Wierix title page more than 300 years earlier.

While these benches were used for a wide variety of tasks (Roubo shows them being used for marquetry), they are more commonly associated with the joiner's trade. Joiners were the people who outfitted a house with all the doors, windows, shutters and trim. They could also be responsible for some of the cabinetry with its doors and drawers. But joiners weren't producing the fancy cabinets with veneer, inlay, marquetry and the like. That was the job of the cabinetmakers.

These timber-framed benches usually had fairly simple workholding. On the benchtop you would have an adjustable planing stop and holes for holdfasts. The front of the bench usually featured a crochet (a hook for planing edges) or a leg vise. These benches rarely have a complex tail vise or a tool tray (though it did happen). Sometimes they would have a sliding deadman to help support big doors or boards when you work their long edges.

Most woodworkers I know (myself included) would fall into the historical category of joiner. We make (by historical standards) pretty simple stuff. The bench's basic workholding and simple construction make it a good choice for joiners.

PROS: Strong and simple joinery doesn't require a high degree of skill. Benches are heavy and can be adapted to be used in a variety of trades.

ALL THE MISTAKES

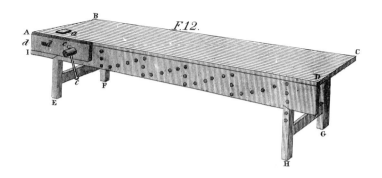

PANELED BENCH, GREAT BRITAIN, EARLY 19ᵀᴴ CENTURY
A WORKBENCH FROM PETER NICHOLSON'S "MECHANICS COMPANION," WHICH USES FAR LESS WOOD THAN A TIMBER-FRAMED WORKBENCH.

CONS: Parts are large and can be difficult to source or dry. Large, thick benchtops can be time-consuming to laminate. Monolithic slabs are prone to warp.

3. PANEL WORKBENCHES

This form of workbench seems to have originated in Great Britain, then it emigrated to the United States. It shows up in the written record in the early 1800s (Peter Nicholson's "The Mechanic's Companion" [1812], though I suspect it might be much older than that). This bench is built using thin and wide panels to create a stiff box. Then it has some thicker components for legs (and sometimes stretchers).

The U-shaped box that creates the benchtop requires much less wood than a timber-framed workbench, a big plus for an island nation that has to import a lot of its timber.

These benches can be assembled with nails, screws or traditional joinery. And the workholding is usually pretty basic. A planing stop is typical on the benchtop. And some sort of screw-driven face vise is typical for the front. The front apron of the bench is typically pierced with holes for pegs or holdfasts, which are used for supporting long stock.

In the U.K., this bench shows up in almost every sort of shop. I've seen it in high-end ateliers and in barns. When this bench emigrated to the United States, it was adopted by the carpentry trade. As the United States turned increasingly to stick-built houses, this bench became the first thing carpenters would build on the job site, using dimensional lumber. Those days are long gone, however. If there's a bench on a job site, it's likely plywood on sawhorses – or a Black & Decker Workmate.

When it comes to simplicity, portability and economy, a paneled bench, which I call a Nicholson bench, cannot be beat. You can build one in two days with just a handful of tools and dimensional lumber. Why isn't this bench my favorite of all time? We'll get to that in a bit.

PROS: Benches are lightweight, inexpensive and easily made with a limited toolkit. Can be made quickly and without any machines and with little wood.

CONS: Front apron can impede some clamping operations. Thin components can warp easily if wet. Bench's light weight can be a liability if the bench is small and can be moved around too easily.

4. BUILT-IN BENCHES

Benches that are built into the structure of the surrounding building have been common for many centuries. It makes economic sense to use your shop's building to help support the workbench. These benches show up frequently in German paintings from the 1600s and are still in use today. Many old houses have a built-in workbench in the garage or basement.

These built-in benches can take many forms. They might have a slab benchtop. Or be made from thin panels. The legs can be made in almost any form – I've even seen trestle-table legs on a built-in bench. The workholding is usually basic – maybe a vise is attached on or below the benchtop.

Who uses these benches? Today I see them mostly in garages where they are used for home maintenance and auto repair. While you can build fine furniture on them, built-in benches can be frustrating because the bench is fixed. You can't pull it to the middle of the shop and work all around it – a plus for all other workbench forms.

ALL THE MISTAKES

BUILT-IN BENCHES, DUXBURY, MASS., 18ᵀᴴ CENTURY
THERE IS A LONG TRADITION (VIRTUALLY IGNORED) OF BUILDING
WORKBENCHES INTO THE STRUCTURE OF THE SURROUNDING BUILDING.

PROS: Bench is economical and stout thanks to affixing it to a building. Can be made easily with almost any toolkit and budget.
CONS: Some workholding operations can be awkward due to the immobility of the bench. Bench cannot be moved without taking it apart.

∧ ∧ ∧

BUILT-INS: THE BENCH THAT'S HARD TO SEE

When I first saw a drawing of an 18th-century French workbench, I was amazed that this bench form had been hiding in plain sight for hundreds of years.

But little did I know how myopic I was.

THE ANARCHIST'S WORKBENCH

Though I'd written two books about old workbenches, I had neglected the workbench form that is likely the most common in North America. In fact, I had actually owned one of these benches in the first house I bought in 1992 with my wife, Lucy, in Lexington, Ky. But somehow that fact didn't register on my brainpan.

When we bought our Victorian cottage on West Sixth Street, I was thrilled by its wooden-frame garage from the early 20th century. I had planned to set up shop there until the termite inspector told me the thing was about to collapse.

So instead, I stored my tools and machines in there, mostly stacked on shelves around the perimeter of the structure. Then I set up shop on the house's back porch (which was stooped over from rot instead of termites).

And that was the end of that workbench story.

Fast forward about 20 years to 2013. Michael Burrey, a restoration carpenter, had discovered an intact 18th-century workshop outside Boston that had been most recently used for storing toys. And I got to visit it.

It was a white clapboard building, and the interior was a time capsule. The bench room was lined with built-in workbenches and evidence – everywhere – that the building had been an active hand-tool workshop.

It hit me that this small shop was similar to my old garage in Lexington – lined with built-in workbenches, shelves and windows. Then I recalled a dozen other basements and garages with similar built-in workbenches. Why had I never thought much about them? Or written a single word?

Built-in workbenches are everywhere. And they deserve some ink because they might be the catalyst that turns a casual DIYer into the next James Krenov.

Modern built-in workbenches are typically made from a frame of butt-jointed 2x4s with a benchtop that is 3/4"-thick construction plywood screwed to the framework. Sometimes the 2x4s form a rectangular box that supports the benchtop. Other times the 2x4s are angled to support the benchtop. You almost always have some shelves above the benchtop that are lined with coffee cans filled with rusty screws and bolts.

If you are lucky, the bench has a vise. Sometimes it is a small

ALL THE MISTAKES

AMERICAN BUILT-IN WORKBENCH, 20ᵀᴴ CENTURY
Many homes with garages or basements feature workbenches attached to the stud-frame walls.

quick-release vise from the hardware store. Other times it is a mechanics' vise bolted to the top of the benchtop.

Surprisingly, the benches at the workshop outside Boston (circa 1789) aren't much different than modern built-in benches. The tops are supported by a simple framework. Legs prop up the benchtops at regular intervals.

What is different about the 18th-century built-ins is that the benchtops are solid wood instead of plywood – likely a thick softwood. And some of the old benches' legs had leg vises and parallel guides. The old shop also had a built-in lathe, which isn't typical in a modern garage. But the walls were lined with shelves and tool racks, a feature that hasn't changed in 230 years.

THE ANARCHIST'S WORKBENCH

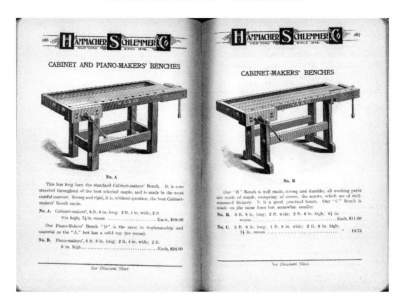

COMMERCIAL CABINETMAKER'S BENCHES, 19TH CENTURY
BY THE 19TH CENTURY, COMPANIES WERE MANUFACTURING WORKBENCHES THAT COULD BE SHIPPED BY RAIL AND ASSEMBLED ON-SITE.

5. CABINETMAKER'S BENCHES

The highest-evolved form of workbench emerged in the late 18th or early 19th century. From a construction point of view, it is ingenious. The base typically is built in the style of a trestle table. It is strong, does not require massive components and usually can be knocked down for transport. The top is usually laminated and wrapped by a skirt that then becomes the rear wall of the tool well. Sometimes these skirts are dovetailed around the benchtop.

The vises are highly refined. The face vise is driven by a screw (usually metal), and its large wooden jaw runs parallel to the benchtop thanks to two steel bars. The tail vise is a moving box, usually dovetailed together, that is powered by a steel screw as well (though wooden versions absolutely exist).

The bench usually has square dogs, either wood or steel. Other common features include a drawer below the benchtop and sometimes holdfast holes (though who needs them with the tail vise?). Gone is the planing stop found on earlier benches (which can leave marks on your work).

This bench form is readily made in a factory. The benchtop can be made from smaller pieces that are glued together instead of one massive slab. And the whole thing comes apart in minutes. The top lifts off the base (it is held by gravity and rests on wooden or steel pins that stick up from the base). So you can pack it flat and ship it.

These benches are ideal for people who do fancy work. They are preferred by woodworkers who do fine joinery, marquetry, carving, chairmaking, veneer and so forth.

Like all workbenches, the quality of these benches depends on the maker or manufacturer. Because this form of bench is so beloved, there are many cheap variations out there that look like the real thing but aren't. When built well, however, this form works like a finely tuned guitar.

PROS: Good examples can hold work firmly for a wide variety of operations. Vises offer simple solutions to many workholding problems. The tool tray is beloved by some.

CONS: Construction is complex. The bench's base is not ideal for working on the edges of large doors or boards. Poorly made examples are misery to work on.

NOW ADD, MIX & COMBINE

So, are you a green woodworker? A joiner? A traditional carpenter? A home DIYer? Or someone who aspires to work at the top of the furniture trade? Once you know that, picking a bench form (and eventually its vises) is more straightforward.

Note that there is a good deal of elasticity in these categories. You can outfit a paneled bench with vises from a cabinetmaker's bench. Or make a built-in workbench that can handle a lot of tasks of a joiner. As you'll see, I stretched these categories myself during the last 20 years as I built (all but two of) the following workbenches.

THE ANARCHIST'S WORKBENCH

THE $175 WORKBENCH, 2020
Despite all its flaws, this workbench has remained a workhorse in my shop and that of my business partner.

THE $175 WORKBENCH (2000)

Benchtop dimensions: 2-7/8" x 26-3/4" x 70"
Materials: Yellow pine
Joinery: Top is laminated. Ends are drawbored mortise-and-tenon joints. Ends are joined with bolts, nuts and washers. Top is attached to the base with long screws through an intermediate cleat.

This is a typical timber-frame bench built with knockdown hardware instead of proper massive joints. The entire bench is made from yellow pine, which is now hard as a rock. The front legs are coplanar to the front edge of the benchtop, which is great for jointing edges and working on the ends of boards. The top is pierced with three rows of 3/4"-diameter dog holes, which were once used with a Veritas Wonder

ALL THE MISTAKES

Dog (a surface-mounted end vise). The top is attached to the base with long screws through thick cleats – not ideal.

In its current form the bench has a Record face vise and a blacksmith-made planing stop. The knockdown hardware has never been knocked down, despite the bench's frequent migrations in Ohio, Indiana and Kentucky.

This poor bench has been changed so much during the last 19 years that it's almost unrecognizable. (Some might say the same thing about me.) Despite its oddness, I still love it. The top has remained remarkably flat through the years, proving the advantage of using a resinous softwood for a benchtop.

It is in many ways almost a copy of the 1580 bench from Hieronymus Wierix's "The Life of the Infant" (though I hadn't seen that bench when I designed this one). If I had to rebuild this bench, it would be much the same, except I would remove all the knockdown hardware and make it with simple mortise-and-tenon joints, like the Wierix bench. I like the Record quick-release vise for the most part, though it's not as versatile as a leg vise.

PROS: It's an inexpensive bench to construct for someone with basic woodworking skills, small-scale woodworking machines and some hand tools. In use, it's easy to clamp work anywhere on the benchtop thanks to its lack of aprons or skirting.

CONS: The knockdown hardware was a pain to install, and I've never had to use it. I wish the benchtop was longer (it's 70" long now – I don't know why). An 8' benchtop would be better.

POWER-TOOL WORKBENCH (2002)

Benchtop dimensions: 2-7/8" x 26" x 53-3/4"
Materials: Yellow pine; plywood for drawer unit
Joinery: Benchtop is laminated. Ends are drawbored mortise-and-tenon joints. Ends are joined with commercial bench bolts from Lee Valley. Top is attached to the base with long screws through steel L-brackets.

I built the power-tool workbench for my home shop, which was small and cramped (thanks to a lot of unnecessary tools). I needed a workbench that was an outfeed table for my table saw, could store

THE ANARCHIST'S WORKBENCH

POWER-TOOL WORKBENCH, 2020 PHOTO
Despite all its workholding options, this bench has become a center for tool and parts storage in our workshop.

some tools and allowed me to do some handwork. I was inspired to build it by Glen Huey, one of our contributing editors at the magazine. He had an old desk behind his table saw that also served as his workbench.

Like the $175 workbench, this bench is a timber-framed form with knockdown hardware. By this time, I had graduated to using fancy bench bolts instead of home center carriage bolts (something I don't plan to repeat in my life – you'll hear a lot more on this in a following chapter). The benchtop and base are yellow pine. The drawer cabinet is made from Baltic birch plywood.

There are lots of things I don't like about this bench. The benchtop is too short (53-3/4"). There initially was no face vise (there is one now) and the twin-screw vise on the end is fussy. I had hoped that the twin-screw would be a do-everything vise. I planned to use it as both a tail vise and as a face vise. That didn't work out. When I used it as a tail vise, it didn't have the grip of a dedicated tail vise with its single screw. As a face vise, it was fine except when I needed to dovetail 24"-wide carcases. I didn't have enough room between the screws (a design flaw on my part).

Also, at the end of the benchtop is a planing stop built with T-track and star knobs. A piece of plywood moves up and down on the end of the bench and is cinched in place with the star knobs. It is surprisingly effective and robust.

Another lesson: The drawer box is always in the way. It interferes with clamping things to the benchtop. And there isn't enough room between the drawer box and the benchtop to use a holdfast. After working with it for a couple years, I set it aside. I later gave it to my father, who needed an outfeed table for his table saw, storage for his tools and a little work area for carving.

It worked great for him, until a hurricane and storm surge left it floating like a cork in his South Carolina garage. All the metal bits rusted, and the wood was covered in black goo. I thought it was a loss. After my dad died, it was one of the few things I took home with me. Surprisingly, I got all the metal parts loose and cleaned of rust. The bench is again in my workshop.

PROS: The best outfeed table I've owned for a table saw. Inexpensive raw materials. Had a lot of lessons to teach me about workbench design. Floats.

CONS: Benchtop is too short. Drawer box is in the way of many operations. Twin-screw is not ideal as a "do everything" vise.

THE 24-HOUR WORKBENCH (2003)

Benchtop dimensions: 3" x 27" x 61"

Materials: The top is Baltic birch plywood edged with yellow pine. The base is yellow pine.

Joinery: The ends are made with drawbored mortise-and-tenon joints. The end assemblies are joined to the long stretchers with commercial bench bolts. The top is joined to the base with screws and 5" L-brackets.

This bench is another child of the $175 Workbench, but it has a plywood top, which is surrounded by yellow pine skirting. I built five or six of these benches while on a traveling woodworking carnival circuit

THE ANARCHIST'S WORKBENCH

24-HOUR WORKBENCH, 2003
This bench features the base from the $175 Workbench with a plywood top, which remained remarkably flat.

with the ShamWow people and the sketchy guys who sold router bits that had "fallen off a truck." At each stop on the circuit my co-workers and I built one of these benches and gave it away in a raffle.

Like its sister, this is a timber-frame bench made with knockdown hardware. The benchtop is the interesting part of the bench. It's made from two sheets of 3/4" Baltic birch plywood ripped down the middle, stacked and glued. You end up with a benchtop that is about 3" x 27" x

60" for about $100. After gluing up one benchtop using clamps, cauls, buckets of water and all our anvils, I got wise. I laminated the top pieces and used screws as clamps, removing the screws after the glue had set up.

The plywood tops were remarkably flat and stayed that way. The least fun part of building the bench was adding the skirting around the top to hide the raw plywood edges. This skirting was joined with finger joints or dovetails, depending on my mood. If I built this bench again, I would skip the skirting and paint the raw plywood edges. Or learn to love raw plywood edges.

The other thing I didn't like about the plywood top was the final flattening. We got these plywood tops quite flat from the get-go. But to get them perfect (whatever that is) I had to handplane them. And occasionally you would plane through the plywood's surface veneer, exposing layers of ugly.

PROS: Dang-flat benchtop that stayed flat. Inexpensive raw materials. Benchtop is easy to glue up with drywall screws and yellow glue.

CONS: Piss ugly. The knockdown hardware is likely unnecessary and adds complexity.

YELLOW PINE ROUBO (2005)

Benchtop dimensions: 4" x 24" x 96"
Materials: Yellow pine; vise jaw is ash
Joinery: Drawbored mortise-and-tenon joinery throughout.

This bench (a true timber-frame bench) was my first brush with ancient forms. It is a reasonable copy of the bench forms shown in Roubo's "l'Art du menuisier," but without the fancy sliding dovetail joint and with lots of redneck yellow pine. I built it using massive mortise-and-tenon joints.

Every joint is drawbored. The workholding on this bench changed through the years. When I first built the bench, I installed a leg vise and a crochet on the front face of the bench (you don't need both, but I wanted to experiment with both). The leg vise was a metal screw, and I added a maple parallel guide. The benchtop had a planing stop (without the metal teeth, at first) plus holes for holdfasts. Later I added a homemade wagon vise. Then I swapped that out for a Benchcrafted tail vise.

WORKBENCH FROM *WOODWORKING MAGAZINE*, 2005
This simple bench, based on what I thought was a French pattern, was my first encounter with ancient workbenches.

ALL THE MISTAKES

2005 WORKBENCH, MODIFIED, 2011 PHOTO
Note that the planing stop doesn't have a metal hook. An early Moxon vise is on the shelf. And a wagon vise is installed as the end vise.

This bench lit a fire under my butt. It was my first peek at what a workbench could really be like. The bench was enormous. And it was blissfully easy to work on. I thought I would have to decode how to work on the bench, but I took to it immediately.

The yellow pine performed admirably, just like it had in the $175 Workbench. After it dried, it became hard and stayed remarkably flat. Though I loved this bench, I sold it after I left the magazine in 2011. My wife and I were freaked out about money at the time (I had just said goodbye to an $80,000 annual salary), and we didn't have room for all my workbenches. I miss this bench.

PROS: Cheap to make. Material is durable and stable. The design (which is not mine) approaches perfection.

CONS: You need a lot of clamps to make the laminated benchtop. And you need some lightweight machines to do the job in weeks instead of months.

THE ANARCHIST'S WORKBENCH

YELLOW PINE PANELED WORKBENCH, 2006
My first paneled workbench, which featured a leg vise and wagon vise. The bench remains in our shop today.

YELLOW PINE NICHOLSON (2006)

Benchtop dimensions: 2-3/8" x 27" x 96"
Materials: Yellow pine; the vise jaw is ash.
Joinery: The top is glued up from three boards to get the top wide enough, plus there are other boards that add thickness. The ends of the base are drawbored mortise-and-tenon joints. The top and the base are connected via the aprons and giant notches in the end assemblies.

This was the second bench featured in my 2007 book "Workbenches: From Design & Theory to Construction & Use." And it was my first workbench built using wide panels. I followed Nicholson's instructions as best I could, but there were still some lessons to be learned.

This bench design is adapted from several old benches from Great Britain and the United States. Its angled legs are unusual, but they didn't really make the project more difficult to build or the bench more stable in use.

The bench has a leg vise for the face vise and a homemade wagon vise for the end vise, which still works remarkably well. The top and front apron are pierced with holes for holdfasts and pegs. After I first built the bench, I added two of the commercial aluminum planing stops, the ones that move up and down with a small thumbscrew. They are hateful things. They are difficult to install and the thumbscrew on one of them snapped within a few weeks. I removed them, patched the mortises and added a wooden planing stop instead.

The most interesting lesson this bench offered was about yellow pine and its limits. The stuff I had used was clear and pretty dry. During this phase of my bench-building life I'd cut the blanks to length and let them dry for a week. That would be dry enough.

Not so with this bench. The wide boards for the benchtop curled up after they were glued up. So there was a lot of flattening to do to get the benchtop working – much more work than my other thick laminated yellow pine tops. Also, I learned that a single layer of yellow pine was not thick enough for a hand-tool benchtop. It was too springy.

So, I added a second layer below the benchtop, which fixed the problem.

In use, I find the front apron frustrating. I clamp work to my benchtop quite a bit, and the apron gets in my way. Sometimes holdfasts are the right solution. Other times I clamp the work between dogs using the wagon vise. But many times, I prefer the direct approach with F-style clamps or bar clamps. This bench, however, does not always cooperate.

This bench currently resides behind my French Oak Roubo workbench, and I use it all the time. It's a good bench, but it's not my all-time favorite.

PROS: Inexpensive materials. Easily and quickly built with hand tools only. Lightweight and easy to move around (but not so light that it lurches during planing).

CONS: Front apron interferes with some clamping operations. The thin benchtop (about 2-3/8") doesn't play well with some commercial holdfasts.

THE ANARCHIST'S WORKBENCH

TIMBER-FRAMED WORKBENCH IN HARDWOOD, 2007
WOEFULLY MISNAMED, THIS WORKBENCH BEARS LITTLE RESEMBLANCE TO THE BENCH SHOWN IN THE HOLTZAPFFEL CATALOG.

HOLTZAPFFEL WORKBENCH (2007)

Benchtop dimensions: 3" x 24-1/8" x 72"
Materials: The top is ash; the base and vise jaw are maple.
Joinery: Mortise-and-tenon joinery throughout.

This bench is a bit of a bastard, design-wise. And it is likely misnamed (my fault). But it is a dang fine workbench with a difficult-to-say name (HOLT-zaff-fell).

The bench has an ash benchtop and a maple base. It is a true timber-framed bench with no knockdown fasteners. When I first built the bench, I installed a wooden twin-screw vise as the face vise and a large quick-release vise as the end vise. This combination seemed ideal. The twin-screw vise would be great for dovetailing and planing boards on edge. The quick-release vise was easier to install than any other end vise I've encountered. Plus it could do some face-vise-like chores.

For the most part, everything worked out.

ALL THE MISTAKES

The design was from a 19th-century text by Charles Holtzapffel, a tool merchant in Great Britain. But I made some (OK, a lot of) changes to his design. In essence, his design showed a fancy knockdown cabinetmaker's bench with a twin-screw face vise. I transformed it into a timber-frame workbench with a twin-screw face vise.

Since building it, the only significant change I've made to the bench is I added a removable leg vise. Now I can swap back and forth between a twin-screw with 24" between the screws (great for dovetailing) and a leg vise (great for everything else). If I could change one thing about the bench it would be to move the row of dog holes closer to the front edge of the benchtop (I plan to make this change some day). Having the dog holes up near the front edge is a great help when using joinery planes with hangy-down fences (such as a plow plane). Oh, I also added a wooden planing stop.

PROS: Stout, versatile and you can clamp almost anything anywhere to the benchtop. Twin-screw vise makes dovetailing easier.
CONS: Dog holes should be closer to the front edge of the top.

LVL WORKBENCH AKA "GLUEBO" (2009)

Benchtop dimensions: 2-1/2" x 24" x 94"
Materials: Laminated veneer lumber (LVL)
Joinery: The top is laminated LVL, as is the base. The base components are joined with lap joints, bolts, washers and nuts. The top is attached to the base via lag screws through the base and into the benchtop.

One of my favorite artists in Charleston, S.C., David Puls, works a lot with laminated veneer lumber (LVL), which is basically jumbo-thickness plywood. After seeing what he could do with the material – it has striking structural properties – it was a short mental hop to use it in a workbench.

There's always a day when you aren't building a workbench that turns into a day when you are. I was eating lunch with the magazine's staff at a new noodle restaurant when Megan Fitzpatrick and I began staring at the restaurant's tabletops. They were made from LVL that had been ripped, turned 90° and glued up. Imagine a tabletop made entirely of the raw edge of plywood.

LAMINATED VENEER LUMBER BENCH, 2009
ONE OF MY MORE EXTREME EXPERIMENTS WITH MATERIALS, THIS WORKBENCH USED LVL THROUGHOUT.

ALL THE MISTAKES

And so that afternoon I began looking for LVL beams so Megan and I could build a workbench.

For me, this was an experiment with a new material, particularly for the benchtop. Would it be as flat as the other plywood benches I had made six years earlier? Would the material be a pain to work with? The bench itself looks like a Roubo bench, but it is a fake. It uses fasteners and half-lap joints in the base. The top is bolted down to the base (a big mistake). The face vise is a leg vise. And we added a small quick-release vise for the end vise.

In my opinion, the LVL worked great for the benchtop. This was definitely a project where machines were necessary; LVL is tough stuff. It was murder on our machines' carbide edges. And it was merciless to the edges of handplanes. But after we glued it into a benchtop, it started flat and has stayed flat to this day.

The base of the bench was (my opinion again) a failure. *[Editor's note: It is not just your opinion.]* Bolting together the base wasn't a good idea. The layers of the LVL were crushed by the bolt heads and washers, making it difficult to get a solid joint. And attaching the top with lag screws wasn't ideal either. The leg vise easily pushed the benchtop off the base in short order.

If I built this bench again, I would use mortise-and-tenon joints throughout – no metal fasteners. That would solve all the problems we encountered.

Despite my dire words above, the bench is still in daily use in our shop. We have made the thing work with shims here and there.

PROS: LVL stays flat in service. After 11 years it is still perfectly flat.

CONS: LVL is hard on your machines and worse on your hand tools. Some people might not like the non-traditional look. Using mechanical fasteners on the base is not a good idea. Though LVL is a non-traditional material, traditional joinery is still the best way to deal with it.

ROUBO WORKBENCH, CHERRY BENCHTOP, 2010
The finish is still drying on this bench when the photo was taken. Note the door hasn't yet been installed over the shelf.

CHERRY SLAB ROUBO (2010)

Benchtop dimensions: 4-3/8" x 18-1/2" x 67"
Materials: The top is two slabs of black cherry. The legs are cottonwood (Populus deltoides). The stretchers are white pine. The current leg vise jaw is maple.
Joinery: The base is constructed with drawbored mortise-and-tenon joinery. The base and top are joined with the French tenon/sliding dovetail.

After experimenting with alternative materials (and bolts, ugh), I was eager to build another true timber-framed bench, this time with traditional materials and traditional tools only. I wanted to make a slab-top workbench as shown in Roubo with the sliding dovetail joint shown in his drawings. This also was my introduction to the world of wet and sometimes rotting slabs for benchtops.

The cherry slab came from woodworker Ron Herman's parking lot. It had been sitting outside for a season or two and had some rot. But it

ALL THE MISTAKES

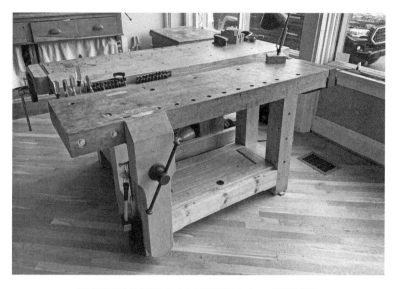

CHERRY ROUBO, MODIFIED, 2020 PHOTO
AFTER 14 YEARS OF HEAVY USE, THIS BENCH HAD A NEW LEG VISE, A TOOL RACK, PLANING STOP AND A STUPID DOOR OVER THE SHELF.

looked like there was enough sound wood to make a benchtop. I made the legs using cottonwood posts from the garden center. The stretchers were white pine.

For workholding, at first I used a leg vise with a parallel guide for the face vise. One day a student cracked the 1-3/4"-thick maple jaw in half while clamping something in the vise. I was shocked. I replaced the vise with a Benchcrafted classic vise and Crisscross. And I made the jaw using 3-1/4"-thick maple (laminated from two layers of 8/4 maple).

For the end vise, I used a vintage Sheldon quick-release vise. The bench features a row of dog holes, a few holdfast holes and a rack on the back edge of the benchtop (a first for me). The planing stop is a vintage metal doohickey from Millers Falls. You adjust it up and down with a screwdriver. It's not an improvement over a blacksmith-made stop, I'm afraid.

Also notable: The shelf has a door covering it. More on that stupid move in a moment.

Building this bench by hand was great fun (except for ripping the top to width). I do miss getting paid to build stuff entirely old school.

This bench offered up many good lessons. Here are some of the important ones.

Rotted slabs are no good for bench building. Even after cutting away all the punky stuff, the cherry had been weakened by its time out in the weather. So, I filled splits and voids with a flexible epoxy used to patch rotten window sills and columns on historic houses. The stuff works well, but there were some unexpected side-effects. Squeeze out was a problem – because it continued for about two years. As the wood moved, the epoxy would bulge out like a vein, and I would have to plane it flat every so often.

Also, one of the rotted bits unexpectedly popped off during a seminar. I bolted it back on.

Mostly, I learned that thick slab benchtops take a long time to dry. Two years isn't enough. In fact, some slabs keep their moisture for more than a decade. And as they dry, they can warp.

Aside from the Millers Falls planing stop, which regularly gets gummed with sawdust, the workholding is fine. It's all stuff that has proven itself many times before.

The silliest thing about the bench is the door that covers the shelf below. I put it there because someone – the magazine's art director, photographer or publisher – thought that the bench needed something "down there" for a photo shoot so it didn't look identical to my earlier benches. I'm a team player, so I made the lid on the morning of the shoot. But it's not a good idea. If you put something in the compartment and close the lid, then you will stack stuff on the lid, making the compartment inaccessible.

I haven't removed the lid. I keep it as a reminder that some bright ideas (and even bright people) should be ignored.

PROS: Slab workbenches are beautiful. The workholding is great. It's a fun bench to build entirely by hand.

CONS: Slabs can be wet, rotten and difficult to move around. Because of rot, this particular benchtop ended up a little narrower and a little shorter than planned at 18-1/2" x 67" (thanks, Saprophytic fungi!*).*

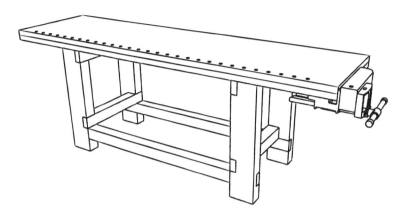

IKEA COUNTERTOP WORKBENCH, 2013
There is something amiss when you cannot find a single photo of a
workbench that you built three times.

IKEA COUNTERTOP WORKBENCH (2013) AKA "TWOBO"
Benchtop dimensions: 3" x 24" x 96"
Materials: Beech benchtop with Douglas fir base.
Joinery: The base is joined with lap joints, bolts, washers and nuts. The top is joined to the base using lag screws.

Soon after quitting my job at *Popular Woodworking*, the magazine asked me to help produce some videos as an independent contractor. I love to eat and was scared to death. So I agreed. One of our first projects was a video titled "Build a Sturdy Workbench in Two Days" (probably the least-snappy video title ever). In this video I built a workbench that used two IKEA countertops to create the benchtop. The base was made by bolting together Douglas fir legs and stretchers. It was similar to the LVL bench above but with a different benchtop. And it had only one vise, a Jorgensen quick-release vise in the end vise position – plus dog holes, of course. And it had a crochet.

Like many of the benches above, this looked like a timber-framed bench but it used metal fasteners for its strength.

Using IKEA countertops for the benchtop seemed a clever move. I first scraped off the film finish from the countertops then glued them together face-to-face to make a 3" x 24" x 96" benchtop from beech (sometimes IKEA sold them in maple). It was fairly cheap – about $300 for the two countertops. It didn't look half bad.

I made a few other benches this way and concluded that IKEA needed to improve quality control. Many of the countertops were not even close to equilibrium as far as moisture content goes. And they were beech – a wood that moves a lot as it dries. So, these countertops would twist and try to pull themselves apart, even when glued and screwed together.

But the core idea – gluing countertops together – is valid. Look around your town for a place that sells or makes butcher block countertops. Visit warehouse stores that sell salvaged building materials. Maple countertops show up frequently, and they can be inexpensive. And if they are salvaged material, they have had plenty of time to dry.

The downside to this approach is only the appearance. Wooden countertops are usually made with short bits of wood that are finger-jointed end-to-end, as well as edge-to-edge. So they look like a patchwork of blocks glued together. To my eye, that looks wrong. But that's me.

The base of the bench was made using Douglas fir 4x4s. The legs and stretchers were joined by lap joints that were secured with bolts, washers and nuts. As mentioned before, I'm not nuts about nuts when it comes to building benches – unless your workbench has to break down to pieces regularly. The nuts were always coming loose on that bench, which was annoying.

PROS: An easy, inexpensive and fast way to create a hardwood benchtop.
CONS: The finger-jointed tops aren't very pretty. Be sure to check their moisture content (or let them dry for a month or two) before laminating the countertops together. The base would be much improved if it were made with mortise-and-tenon joinery.

ALL THE MISTAKES

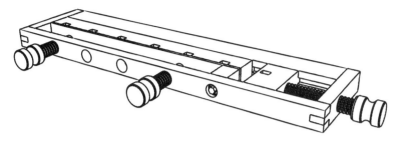

MILKMAN'S WORKBENCH, 2013
A PORTABLE WORKBENCH BASED ON A COMMERCIAL PRODUCT SOLD IN EUROPE,
THIS BENCH IS IDEAL FOR SMALL PROJECTS.

MILKMAN'S WORKBENCH (2013)

Benchtop dimensions: 1-1/2" x 7-5/16" x 30-1/8"
Materials: Maple
Joinery: The top is a laminated construction with a finger-jointed (and pegged) skirt around it. There is no base.

    This portable bench is essentially a cabinetmaker's bench without a base. It is a portable benchtop that you can clamp to a table or countertop. Made using maple, the bench features a wagon vise with square dogs in the end vise position. And the face vise is a series of wooden screws that press the work against the benchtop. I built several Milkman Workbenches in 2013 for customers, and the bench is now made commercially (not by me).
    This is not a substitute for a full-size bench. It was marketed in Denmark as a bench for woodworkers who didn't have a workshop. A woodworking friend in Denmark owned the original bench, which he had obtained from his local milkman – hence the name.
    It's not a bad little workbench for someone who lives in an apartment, who vacations in a recreational vehicle or makes small stuff. One caution: When you build miniature things, you'll find they aren't faster or easier to build than the full-size thing. The joinery is demanding. And the wagon vise has to be precisely built to work properly and survive the long haul.

THE ANARCHIST'S WORKBENCH

PROS: Portable, lightweight and surprisingly useful.
CONS: Too small for most full-size furniture work. The bench is demanding to construct (but the results are rewarding).

FRENCH OAK ROUBO PROJECT BENCH (2013)
Benchtop dimensions: 5-1/4" x 21-1/2" x 95-1/2"
Materials: Oak throughout.
Joinery: The base is joined with drawbored mortise-and-tenon joints. The top is joined to the base using the French tenon/sliding dovetail joint.

In 2012, Father John and Jameel Abraham at Benchcrafted approached me about an idea they had. A woodworker and importer named Bo Childs had some enormous slabs of French oak that had been drying for 13 years or so. What if we got a bunch of people together at Bo's shop in Georgia and built some French benches with these slabs?

I couldn't say "yes" fast enough.

In July of 2013, we put on the first French Oak Roubo Project (FORP) in Barnesville, Ga. This wasn't the first time I had worked with big slabs, but it was the first time I had done it with a big group of people in a commercial shop.

Thanks to that first FORP (and two subsequent FORPs and writing a book with three slab-based workbenches), I've learned a lot about building workbenches with giant slabs – think 6" thick x 24" wide x 96" long (or longer). The bench I use every day in my Kentucky shop was the result of the first FORP, so I do love the form. But slabs have downsides.

But first, the good stuff.

Huge, single-piece slabs make the most beautiful workbenches. Because big slabs aren't perfect, they look like the antique benchtops I've seen in Europe. Knots, voids, splits – that's how the old benches look. If you don't like defects, stay away from slabs. My FORP bench has seen seven years of hard use and looks better than the day I finished it.

Once the massive tops release a lot of moisture, they move very little. When we first cut into the 6"-thick slabs the interiors were shock-

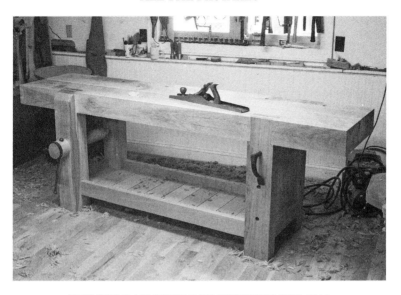

FRENCH OAK ROUBO PROJECT BENCH, 2013
Built using giant slabs of oak, this series of workbenches offered lessons on dealing with wet stock.

ingly wet. One moisture meter recorded 60 percent. That's too wet for yellow glue.

We quickly learned that the so-called "rules" for drying lumber don't apply to thick slabs. In some cases, 13 years is not long enough. So, what do you do?

Our approach was to use the driest slabs in the stack. Then cut the joinery and assemble the components as quickly as possible. If you dally, your components will move. Parts that once fit perfectly will not fit at all.

Once you get the bench assembled, you have to endure some wood movement. The good news is that assembled benches – with a firm framework below – tend to stay flatter than slabs that are unrestrained. The legs and stretchers restrain the top (in my experience). The top shrinks around the joints, which helps hold the four corners of the benchtop in the same plane.

The top will shrink quite a bit once you get the bench into a climate-controlled workshop. If you used through-tenons to join the top and base, you will need to plane down the ends of the tenons regularly. I suspect my FORP benchtop lost almost 1/4" of thickness in its first three years.

Wait, don't run away just yet. There's a happy ending to the story. Once the top dries, it hardly moves at all. For the last two years the top hasn't moved much – maybe 1/64". I love it.

The downsides to using a single slab are mostly the difficulty of working with one in a small workshop by yourself. A 6" x 22" x 96" oak benchtop that is filled with water is difficult for one person to move around. Assembling it yourself takes planning (I've done it several times, however). Moving the finished bench in and out of a building requires assistance.

The wetness of the slab can also interfere with your glue. If you have to glue up two slabs to make your benchtop, the slabs might be too wet for yellow glue (PVA) or animal glue. You might have to use epoxy. And though I use epoxy quite a bit, it requires some care. You have to mix it well. And sometimes you get a bad batch (which we did at the second FORP).

Part of me contends that if you are after a slab workbench then you should use a single-piece top because there won't be a difficult glue-up to do. But the other half of me knows that a single flatsawn slab is more likely to twist than almost any laminated top.

No matter what you decide, make sure the top doesn't have the pith running through it. It will split, and the split could be fatal.

Despite all the downsides listed above, I still enjoy building slab workbenches. But I do it with a forklift, pneumatic mortiser, 24" Martin planer and a group of people with sturdy backs.

PROS: One of the most gorgeous benches I've made. Mass in spades.
CONS: Wet slabs can twist, even years later.

KNOCKDOWN NICHOLSON (2015)

Benchtop dimensions: 2-1/4" x 22-1/2" x 72"
Materials: Yellow pine
Joinery: The top is laminated. The ends are joined with lap joints and screws. The remainder of the bench is assembled with 3/8" bolts and T-nuts.

KNOCKDOWN PANELED BENCH UNDER CONSTRUCTION, 2015
Though the construction is clever, I prefer a bench that doesn't require metal fasteners for stability.

While I broadly prefer the timber-framed bench form, I have a soft region in my heart for the Nicholson workbench. It requires about half the material of a French bench of the same size. It can be screwed together and be sturdy (Mike Siemsen proved that in his "Naked Woodworker" videos).

I wanted to make a version that was knockdown in preparation for teaching a class on the form in the U.K. (And it – cough, cough – made for a good magazine article and cover photo.)

The bench was made using yellow pine and was held together with oversized T-nuts, bolts, washers and wood screws. The whole thing came apart to pieces in a few minutes with a ratchet set. Other than that, it was a standard Nicholson bench that would wobble if you didn't keep the bolts snug.

The workholding was basic: A crochet on the front face of the bench and a planing stop on the benchtop. There were holes for holdfasts and pegs on the benchtop and front apron.

THE ANARCHIST'S WORKBENCH

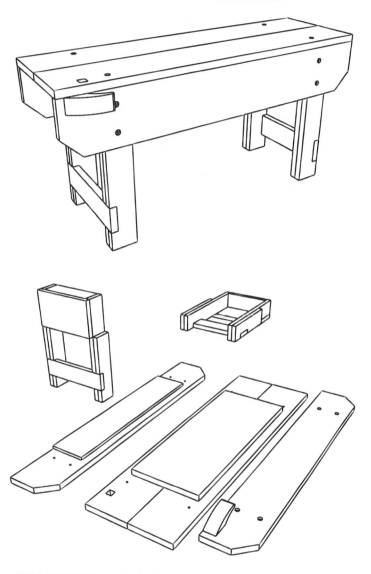

KNOCKDOWN NICHOLSON, CONSTRUCTION DRAWING
THE WORKBENCH IS EASILY CONSTRUCTED WITHOUT ANY COMPLEX JOINERY, WHICH IS ITS PRIMARY ADVANTAGE AND FLAW.

ALL THE MISTAKES

HERCULANEUM WORKBENCH, 2016
An eight-legged workbench based on a destroyed Roman fresco.

PROS: Cheap to build (especially if you omit the T-nuts and bolts and just screw it together). And it can be moved easily in almost any vehicle.

CONS: It's a little small (the top is 22-1/2" x 72"). And like its full-size brother, the apron gets in the way of clamping things to the benchtop at times. Also, I wish I had joined the lower stretchers and legs with a full mortise-and-tenon joint instead of notches and screws. The joints didn't come loose, but they aren't ideal for the long haul.

HERCULANEUM WORKBENCH (2016)
Benchtop dimensions: 3" x 15" x 85"
Materials: oak
Joinery: Staked. Round tenons wedged into the benchtop.

If you thought "Holtzapffel" was a mouthful, stay tuned.
During research into early bench forms, I searched for the earliest

workbench. No one has turned up a convincing Egyptian workbench to my knowledge. So the earliest benches I know of are images recovered from the Italian cities of Herculaneum and Pompeii, which were destroyed by the eruption of Mt. Vesuvius in 79 C.E.

What was different about these staked workbenches was how low they were – about chair-height. You sit on them while working. This bench form survives to this day but not in cabinetmaking shops. The low bench is still found in some chairmaking shops, and it is widely used in rural crafts. I also contend that the shaving horse is a low bench with a foot-activated clamp.

One bench illustrated in a now-degraded fresco at Herculaneum was the bench that called to me. It had eight (!) legs and was drawn with a holdfast.

A second bench drawing from Pompeii (which survives to this day) shows a four-legged bench. The only workholding shown on the Pompeii bench is nails. The woodworker at the bench (named Perdix) has restrained a leg or post on the benchtop by wedging it between nails driven into the bench. And he is mortising the workpiece. This detail is particularly amazing because a similar wedging action is shown in a chairmaker's bench from the 18th century (M. Hulot's "L'Art du Tourneur Mécanicien" from 1775). And even in chairmakers' benches from the 20th century (Chester Cornett and Dallas Bump, among others).

I built the Herculaneum bench so that I could be the first guy in Covington with an eight-legged bench. I had a blacksmith, Peter Ross, make the Roman holdfast, which looks like a candy cane. I also added a series of holes in the benchtop for pegs (and the holdfast). The pegs were used for restraining the work on its face and on edge. There are also two adjustable wooden planing stops at one end.

Later I added an early style face vise that had wooden screws affixed in the benchtop and a movable chop that was secured with hurricane-shaped nuts.

As mentioned earlier, the Herculaneum bench is great for a lot of tasks where you sit – planing and mortising especially. And crosscutting and ripping with full-size saws is a joy. I have yet to find a way to cut dovetails or tenon cheeks on it that is as easy as with a tall bench. But I'll keep looking.

LÖFFELHOLZ WORKBENCH, 2016
This Germanic bench features a Roman-style base with modern vises. Designed in 1505.

PROS: *Can be built in a day. Ideal for many green woodworking tasks. It also is an excellent sitting bench or coffee table when placed in a living area.*
CONS: *Not ideal for high-class joinery such as dovetails.*

LÖFFELHOLZ WORKBENCH (2016)
Benchtop dimensions: 4-1/4" x 19" x 83-1/2"
Materials: Oak
Joinery: Staked construction. Wedged round tenons staked to the benchtop.

The second staked bench I built was a copy of the first known "modern" workbench, which was illustrated in a 1505 codex by Martin Löffelholz. The bench is the first image of a bench that has a tail vise, a face vise (a twin-screw no less) and a series of dogs.

THE ANARCHIST'S WORKBENCH

Unlike a modern bench, however, the benchtop sits on four tapered legs that are staked into the top. They splay out like the legs of a chair, with no stretchers between the legs. The tail vise and dog system uses iron bits that are filed with sharp teeth. The teeth hold the work tenaciously, but they also mark the end grain of your work. The twin-screw vise uses hand-threaded screws that are glued into the benchtop. The vise's moving jaw clamps tight with two wooden nuts. I also cut two open notches in the benchtop. These notches allow you to wedge work in place (there is more information on these notches in the section on vises).

All the workholding on this bench works as well as any modern gear, and the bench is a 500-year-old design.

The entire bench was built with red oak that was fairly wet. It seemed as wet as the French oak slabs we used in Georgia. When I drilled the mortises with an electric drill, for example, we had to stop because it looked like the wood had caught fire. There was a huge cloud of smoke billowing from the hole. It wasn't fire. The cloud turned out to be steam from the moisture in the wood.

I finished the bench. It works great. The cranked wagon vise is very effective. And the twin-screw vise works perfectly. The problem was that the top twisted. Badly. Unlike the French oak benches, this bench has four independent legs that weren't restrained by stretchers below. Two of the corners of the benchtop bent up. Two bent down. The bench still works fine for many operations, but visually, the thing is a mess. One of the legs is propped up more than 1" to keep the whole shebang from rocking.

I now have the bench in my living room. I use it when we run classes in my workshop below and I need a quiet place to work. If I ever build another, I'll be sure to use drier wood. The main lesson here is: If you use wet wood, you are taking a risk. To reduce that risk, stretchers are a great idea.

PROS: Though it's a staked bench, it has elements of a cabinetmaker's bench and can be used for fine work.

CONS: You need to have the hardware for the tail vise made by a blacksmith. Adding a shelf below the benchtop is not as simple as with benches with plumb legs.

ALL THE MISTAKES

SAALBURG WORKBENCH, 2017
BASED ON THE OLDEST EXTANT WORKBENCH, THIS LOW BENCH FEATURES
SIMPLE WORKHOLDING AND TWO MYSTERIOUS NOTCHES.

THE ANARCHIST'S WORKBENCH

SAALBURG WORKBENCH (2017)

Benchtop dimensions: 3-7/16" x 11" x 101"
Materials: Oak
Joinery: Wedged mortise-and-tenon joinery throughout.

The other low and staked workbench I built was based on the oldest surviving workbench known. It resides at a restored Roman fort in Saalburg, Germany (circa 187 C.E.). I measured the original and built a fairly close copy of it in my shop in Kentucky.

The Saalburg bench has four legs joined to the benchtop with square mortise-and-tenon joints. The bench features a planing stop that likely had an iron tooth (blacksmith Peter Ross made mine based on a stop recovered from Saalburg). And there are two notches on one long edge of the bench – vaguely dovetailed shaped (it's difficult to tell exactly because the bench was submerged in a well for hundreds of years).

In addition to the Roman workholding, I added a removable clamping system that turned the bench into an effective shaving horse. I added a V-shaped Chinese planing stop (called a palm) that was adjustable up and down. (I also added a palm that was nailed down.) Oh, I almost forgot, I added a stop that chairmakers used to shave legs with the assistance of a bib (which was shown in Hulot).

The Saalburg bench is functionally similar to the Herculaneum bench (aside from the accessories I added). What I love about these low benches is how adaptable they are. The book "Woodworking in Estonia" shows them in use by a variety of trades, from coopers to furnituremakers to wheelwrights. They are a blank canvas for exploration, and there is a lot more exploring to be done.

PROS: Easy to build. Works in a variety of situations (including as a sitting bench at Thanksgiving, minus the planing stop). Great for carpentry and green woodworking tasks.

CONS: A little more difficult to build than the Herculaneum bench because of the square, compound-angled mortises. As mentioned before, low workbenches are not the easiest bench for cutting dovetails.

ALL THE MISTAKES

COMMERCIAL CABINETMAKER'S BENCH, 1970s
This Ulmia workbench represents the pinnacle of manufactured workbenches during the 20TH century.

ULMIA WORKBENCH (1970s)

Benchtop dimensions: 3-7/8" x 18-3/8" (plus a 7" tool tray) x 90"
Materials: Beech
Joinery: The top is laminated. The base is assembled with long threaded steel rods, washers and nuts. How the top is attached is unclear.

I own a vintage Ulmia workbench and keep it in the shop. Some students prefer this bench; other visitors like to try it out before they decide which form of bench to build for themselves.

This Ulmia is about as nice an example of a cabinetmaker's bench you can buy. It eclipses all the cheap commercial benches I've tried. (It's on par with the high-quality workbenches from Benchcrafted, Lie-Nielsen Toolworks and Plate 11 Bench Co..) The bench is heavy. The tail vise and face vise are solidly constructed and are driven by nice metal screws.

It has a tool tray, so the working area of the benchtop is small – too small. And the base is the trestle form found on many cabinetmaker's benches. The legs are tenoned into the sled feet to create end assemblies. The two end assemblies are joined with wide stretchers. These are bolted together. I've had to tighten the bolts a couple times.

Aside from the tool tray, the other feature I dislike is the enormous tilting bin below its benchtop. It's supposed to be like having a tool chest below the benchtop that can hold an entire complement of hand tools (if fitted out properly). I honestly think it's a nuisance. We store appliances and the typical shop gear in there. And it doesn't hold much of that.

The only modifications I've made to this bench are adding holes for holdfasts, and I built out the right-hand leg of the bench so it is flush with the benchtop. This allows us to hold doors and long boards with the help of a stout wooden peg.

PROS: Nice vises. Stout construction.

CONS: Expensive to buy or to build. Cheaper versions aren't worth buying. The tool tray reduces the effective benchtop area. The tilting tool bin is not as effective as a simple shelf.

WILL MYERS' MORAVIAN WORKBENCH (2019)

Benchtop dimensions: 3-1/4" x 13-3/4" (plus a 10"-wide tool tray) x 72-3/4"

Materials: Oak benchtop. Yellow pine base and tool tray.

Joinery: The top is a single slab. The ends of the base are joined with mortise-and-tenon joints and lap-dovetail joints. The ends are joined to the long stretchers using tusk tenons. The top and tool tray rest on pegs poking up from the base.

Will Myers built this workbench after a Moravian workbench at Old Salem Museum and Gardens in North Carolina. I consider this bench a hybrid of a timber-frame workbench with some features of a cabinetmaker's workbench – particularly the fine vises and tool tray. The top is a single slab of oak, which is prone to warping like all slabs (ours warped, but that's easily fixed with – duh – woodworking tools).

The tool tray to the rear of the top is capacious, which is a plus or

ALL THE MISTAKES

MORAVIAN BENCH BY WILL MYERS, 2019
A FULLY FEATURED CABINETMAKER'S BENCH THAT KNOCKS DOWN IN MINUTES.

minus, depending on how you look at the world. The base is solid. The end assemblies are tenoned together. Then the entire base is joined with stretchers that are secured with tusk tenons. Tusk tenons are ancient and awesome technology.

They can come loose at times and need to be knocked home in my experience. Keep up with the maintenance and your bench will never sway.

The workholding is highly effective. The bench features a leg vise with Benchcrafted hardware, including a Crisscross. The end vise is a wagon vise, which Myers manufactures, that is simple and effective.

It's an excellent bench, particularly if you need portability. The bench knocks down in minutes. The knockdown capacity is a minus for me, however. We move benches all the time and lifting this one to move it across the shop is always a juggle. The top and tool tray come loose. (We're going to remedy this soon.)

As far as functionality goes, the bench is a winner. I wish it didn't have a tool tray, but that might be because I make a lot of chairs. When you try to stand a chair on a bench with a tool tray, life is no fun.

CONCLUSION

For my work, the best form for a workbench is four chunky legs joined by four stretchers that are paired with a massive benchtop. I try to avoid metal hardware for joinery and use square mortise-and-tenon joints. Preferably drawbored. The front edge of the benchtop should be co-planar with the front legs of the bench. There should be nothing that stops you from clamping work to the benchtop. No aprons, doors, drawers or other awkward (but well-intentioned) stuff.

The workbench form you choose might be different than mine. But no matter which form you pick (or if you attempt to mate Mr. Nicholson and Mr. Löffelholz), the next step is to contemplate the joinery, set out the dimensions of your bench and pick your vises.

ALL THE MISTAKES

LIE-NIELSEN WORKBENCH, 2012
While I prefer to build my workbenches, there are excellent commercial models available, including benches from Lie-Nielsen, Benchcrafted and Plate 11 Bench Co.

FRONTISPIECE TO 'LIFE OF THE INFANT,' C. 1580
HIERONYMUS WIERIX (1553-1619) OF ANTWERP WAS THE SON OF A CABINETMAKER AND PRODUCED THIS REALISTIC DRAWING OF A WORKBENCH AND THE ASSOCIATED TOOLS.

CHAPTER V
BEFORE A.J. ROUBO

A.J. ROUBO'S workbench from "l'Art du menuisier" (1774) is likely the most famous of what I call the "timber-framed" benches – a workbench with a massive benchtop on top of a base constructed using square mortise-and-tenon joints. Four square stretchers join the four legs and (usually) support a shelf.

But this French bench was not the first image of a timber-framed bench, not by at least 200 years. That footnote might belong to someone in Antwerp or maybe a carver in Paris. In fact, the more that researcher Suzanne Ellison and I dig into the historical record, the less certain we are about the origin of the timber-framed bench.

After much discussion, Suzanne and I think there are four epicenters of workbench innovation between the 15th and 18th centuries. In the Low Countries, France and Italy, this squared-off form of workbench appears in engravings, paintings and misericords (a wooden seat for church choir members that can feature a carving below). In addition to those three places, we offer a nod to Nürnberg as one of the epicenters of workbench technology because that is where many of the advanced bench vises seem to originate.

ANTWERP & THE LOW COUNTRIES

We begin about 1565 in St. John's Church (Sint-Janskerk) in the town of Gouda in the Netherlands. In the choir of the church was an altarpiece that shows the four carpentry trades. In one of the panels, there's a workbench (on the next page) with unusual characteristics.

The bench has six vertical legs that appear to be joined to the top with a lapped dovetail joint. Only one pair of legs has a stretcher. There's a planing stop, holes for holdfasts and pegs. While it seems an unlikely construction, there are multiple examples of benches with square legs without stretchers extant. It's easy to speculate that this form of bench was a transitional one between staked, Roman-style benches and the final timber-framed form with four square legs and four square stretchers.

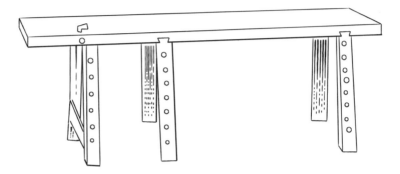

ALTARPIECE ST. JOHN'S CHURCH, GOUDA
A c. 1565 WORKBENCH WITH SIX LEGS AND ONE STRETCHER.

Then, about seven years later, Hans Vredeman de Vries (1527-circa 1607) published a fanciful print, "Panoplia sev armamentarium," which shows tools from four trades, and he drew a full-on timber-framed bench. Though the bench is partially hidden by a lathe and is drawn at a radical tilted angle, his workbench is remarkable. It has fully squared parts, four stretchers, a planing stop, an unusual holdfast and a crochet. Vredeman de Vries was an architect, painter and engineer. His engraving is dated 1572.

The most realistic drawing of the timber-framed workbench and its associated tools was made by Hieronymus Wierix (1553-1619) of Antwerp, the son of cabinetmaker Anton Wierix I (circa 1520/25-circa 1572). Hieronymus and his brother, Johannes Wierix, were wunderkind engravers with long careers of producing religious scenes and portraits. (This plate is shown on the opening page of this chapter.)

Despite their theological bent, the brothers had reputations as drinkers who threw away their money and abandoned commissions, according to the description of their work at the RKD (Rijksbureau voor Kunsthistorische Documentatie), the Netherlands Institute for Art History.

Hieronymus also spent about two years in prison for murder "as he had wounded a certain Clara van Hove's head after several drinks, so that she came to die," according to the RKD's account. He was par-

BEFORE A.J. ROUBO

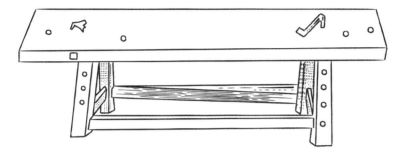

'PANOPLIA SEV ARMAMENTARIUM,' 1572
A WORKBENCH DRAWN BY HANS VREDEMAN DE VRIES (1527-C. 1607) WITH
FOUR LEGS AND FOUR STRETCHERS.

doned in 1580.

Sometime between 1580 and 1610, Hieronymus produced a series of 12 engravings titled "Jesu Christi Dei Domini. Salvatoris Nri Infantia," commonly translated "The Life of the Infant Jesus Christ." The book shows the young Christ child performing a variety of woodworking chores: sawing timbers, building a boat, drilling holes, making a wooden fence, constructing the roof of a house and playing with soap bubbles in his father's woodworking shop.

These images are a goldmine of woodworking information. Hieronymus's father was a cabinetmaker, so the representations of the tools, appliances and workbenches are far more realistic than usual. There's a low bench with a holdfast in the carpentry scene. The image of Joseph's workshop is awash in tools, plus there's a peek at a corner of a timber-framed workbench.

But the most important image is the book's title page, an image I have published many times during the last 13 years and have stared at for hours. It shows dozens of woodworking tools in great detail. And front and center is a timber-framed bench, with both a holdfast and a metal planing stop. (Oh, it also shows the first image of a Dutch slant-lid tool chest that I'm aware of.)

Another contemporary engraver in Antwerp, Joannes Galle (1600-1676), showed two timber-framed workbenches in his engraving

'JOZEF EN CHRISTUS IN DE WERKPLAATS,' C. 1633
THIS ENGRAVING (LIKELY BY JOANNES GALLE) SHOWS ONE BENCH WITH STRETCHERS AND ONE WITHOUT.

BEFORE A.J. ROUBO

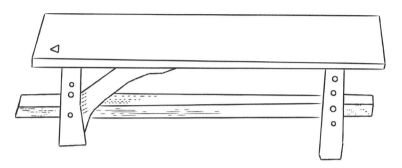

FRENCH MISERICORD, C. 1492-1500
This drawing, based on a carving, suggests this bench might have had some sort of an undercarriage, though it is unclear.

"Jozef en Christus in de werkplaats." The young Jesus is shown planing a board on a timber-framed workbench that doesn't have stretchers. But Joseph's bench seems to have stretchers. So clearly the benches in the Low Countries are in flux during the 16th century. Do we want stretchers? Or are we fine without them?

MEANWHILE, EN FRANÇAIS

About 200 miles from the Antwerp artists, the French were having a similar debate while carving images of workbenches for the misericords for their churches and cathedrals. From the Chapel of St. Lucien de Beauvais (in northern France) there is a misericord carving (circa 1492-1500) of a woodworker planing on a thigh-high workbench. It may or may not have stretchers reinforcing its squared legs.

There is a long plank – longer than the bench – below the benchtop that could be interpreted as part of an undercarriage. Or it could be just a piece of wood below the bench. There also is a curved structure that joins a front leg to the benchtop. This also could be evidence of an undercarriage. Or it could be a piece of wood that the carver left there to strengthen the relief carving itself. The bench definitely has squared-off components, plus a planing stop and holes for pegs or holdfasts in the legs. The misericord now resides at the Musée de Cluny in Paris.

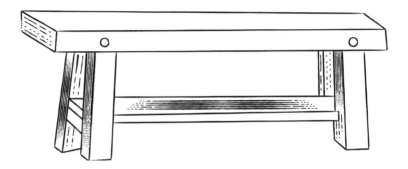

CHURCH OF ST.-GERMAIN, PRESLES, FRANCE
THIS 16TH-CENTURY BENCH SHOWS A SHELF AND LIKELY TWO STRETCHERS, CREATING PART OF AN UNDERCARRIAGE.

Meanwhile, at L'église Saint-Germain-l'Auxerrois, north of Paris, we have a bench with a shelf and at least a partial undercarriage. The bench shows squared-off legs that are clearly tenoned and pegged into the benchtop. Below the top there is a shelf that rests on a stretcher between two of the legs. Sources disagree on an exact date for the misericords in this church. They could be as early as the late 15th century or as late as the mid-16th century.

By the 17th century (but still 100 years before Roubo) this form of timber-framed workbench is common. André Félibien's "Des Principes de L'architecture" (1676–1690) was published about 100 years after Wierix's "Life of the Infant," and yet it shows a virtually identical bench. It has the same overall proportions. The same overhang of the top over the base. A metal planing stop. A holdfast. The only significant difference is that the Félibien image shows additional holdfast holes in the top and front legs.

IN ITALY

In Italy, the birthplace of the staked Roman-style workbench, there is also innovation.

Half a continent away, Francesco Vanni (1563-1610) from Siena, Italy, painted "The Holy Family with Saint Anne in the Carpenter

BEFORE A.J. ROUBO

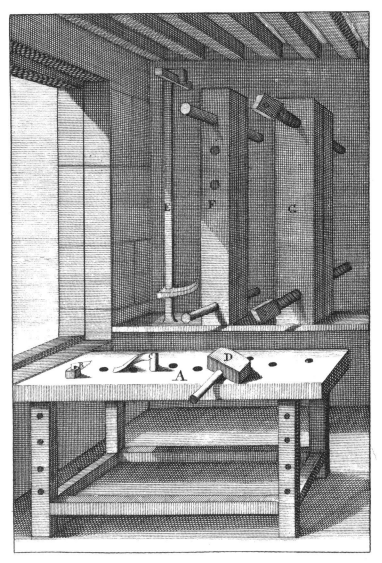

'DES PRINCIPES DE L'ARCHITECTURE' (1676–1690)
André Félibien's workbench is nearly identical to the Wierix bench from 100 years earlier.

THE ANARCHIST'S WORKBENCH

'HEILIGE FAMILIE' 1597, AFTER FRANCESCO VANNI
THIS ENGRAVING, BASED ON A VANNI PAINTING, SHOWS A WORKBENCH WITH ANGLED STRETCHERS.

Shop" in 1583. (Shown is a 1597 engraving based on that painting.) The scene in Joseph's workshop shows a workbench with squared-off legs that are tenoned through the benchtop with square tenons. Plus it has a holdfast almost identical to the Wierix holdfast. But instead of stretchers joined at 90° to the legs, the bench's stretchers are squared off but angled and likely – based on the cross-hatching – joined to the legs with what could be a dovetailed half-lap joint.

IN GERMANY

In the Germanic countries, the timber-framed workbench form was betrothed to the region's mechanical minds. Complex screw vises that showed up around Nürnberg in the early 1500s (via a codex drawn by Martin Löffelholz) and were eventually added to the square

BEFORE A.J. ROUBO

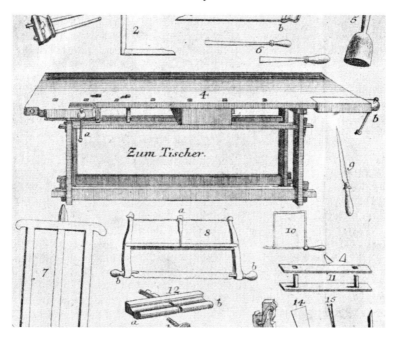

'WERKSTÄTTE DER KÜNSTE,' 1764

GERMANIC COUNTRIES WERE KNOWN FOR THEIR ADVANCED VISES. THE FIRST TAIL VISE WAS ILLUSTRATED IN A 1505 NÜRNBERG CODEX.

timber-framed form.

In Hallens' "Werkstätte der Künste" (or "Workshop of the Arts," 1764) we find a bench built with tusk tenons and through-mortises. And it features many advanced bits of workholding – a tail vise with a system of dogs and a shoulder vise.

Dr. Johann Georg Krünitz's "Ökonomische Encyklopädie" (or "Economic Encyclopedia," a 242-volume work published between 1773-1858) illustrated three interesting workbenches in a 1781 volume. One is clearly a French timber-framed workbench with through-tenons.

This bench has everything. A planing stop and crochet (which are on the right end of the benchtop, suggesting this image was copied from an earlier French source – Jean-Antoine Nollet's "L'Art des

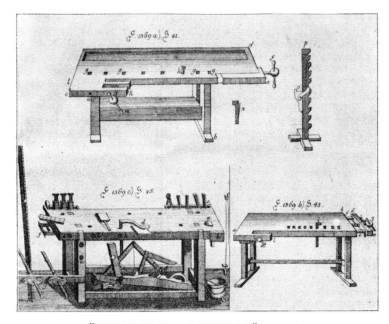

'ÖKONOMISCHE ENCYKLOPÄDIE,' 1781

Dr. Johann Georg Krünitz's multi-volume work showed a variety of workbench forms in use in the 18th century.

expériences – Volume 1," 1770, plate 1). A removable twin-screw vise. A holdfast with a doe's foot. Plus two tool racks.

The other two benches have trestle bases and are fully featured cabinetmaker's benches. Both have end vises, shoulder vises and a system of dogs. One has a tool tray. And these illustrations share a bench slave (as a community, we have got to come up with a better name for this appliance).

AND THEN M. ROUBO

About the same time in France, we have A.J. Roubo, a joiner who learned to draw in order to make the copperplate engravings for his books. He produced more than a dozen images of workbenches for "l'Art du menuisier."

BEFORE A.J. ROUBO

'L'ART DU MENUISIER,' PLATE 50, 1774
A.J. ROUBO SHOWED A VARIETY OF WORKBENCHES IN HIS MULTI-VOLUME
WORK, INCLUDING THIS SIMPLE EXAMPLE WITHOUT A CROCHET.

While the bench shown in Roubo's plate 11 is the image we think of when we think of Roubo, there are other variations sprinkled throughout the books. In plate 50, Roubo shows cherubs working on a 100-percent Wierix bench. No fancy dovetailed joint to bring the top and base together. No crochet. Just a planing stop and holdfast holes.

Many of the other drawings of workbenches resemble the benches drawn by Wierix. No crochet. Just a strong table with blind mortise-and-tenon joints and a planing stop. Sometimes there are holdfast holes (plates 17, 296 and 300) but other times there are not (plate 299). In plate 334, Roubo shows a workbench with a single through-tenon joining the top and base, plus what might be a blind sliding dovetail joint. And the bench for sawing veneer (plate 278) is also a Wierix-style bench with blind joints throughout.

THE ANARCHIST'S WORKBENCH

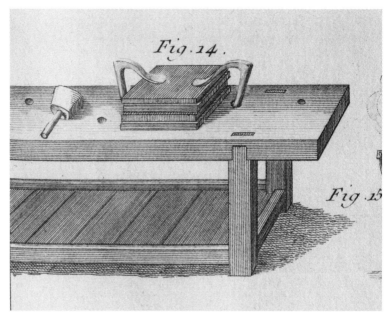

'L'ART DU MENUISIER,' PLATE 334, 1774
IN THIS WORKBENCH, ROUBO SHOWS A VARIATION ON THE JOINT THAT BRINGS
THE BENCHTOP AND THE BASE TOGETHER.

In addition to the simpler benches there's plate 279, where Roubo illustrates his technologically advanced "German" workbench. It features a sliding deadman mated with a leg vise, plus a tail vise and square metal dogs. It has blind joints throughout.

It would be easy to chalk up all these different workbenches in "l'Art du menuisier" to artistic license, but that doesn't give sufficient credit to Roubo, who personally drew almost all of the plates in the five-volume work. The more likely explanation is that Roubo was aware of other forms of workbenches (he interviewed many people in the trades for his books and illustrates workbench variants for caning operations and garden woodwork). I suggest Roubo was simplifying his illustration chores at times and showing forms that existed at the time. Just like when you read a comic book, every car shown in the book isn't a

BEFORE A.J. ROUBO

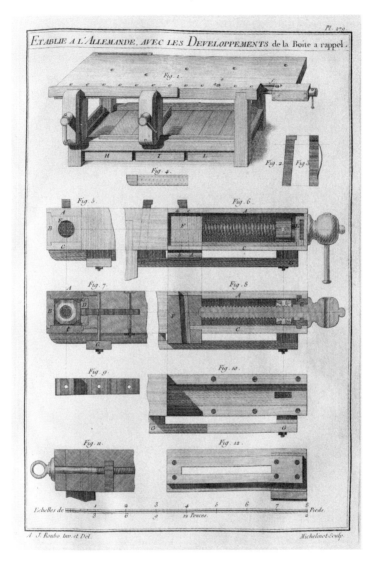

'L'ART DU MENUISIER,' PLATE 279, 1774
The most complex bench shown in A.J. Roubo's text. It is described as a "German workbench."

silver Toyota Camry.

Similarly, the benches shown in Denis Diderot's "Encyclopédie" (1751-1777) show a variety of benches. Most of them look straight out of Wierix's title page – a strong table where the top overhangs the base a little, plus holdfasts and sometimes a crochet.

What does this all mean? I think the benches drawn by Wierix, Vredeman de Vries and others raise interesting questions. Did the timber-framed bench come from the Low Countries, France or somewhere else?

We suspect there are earlier timber-framed benches out there in paintings, engravings or woodcuts in a museum. And so, the search continues.

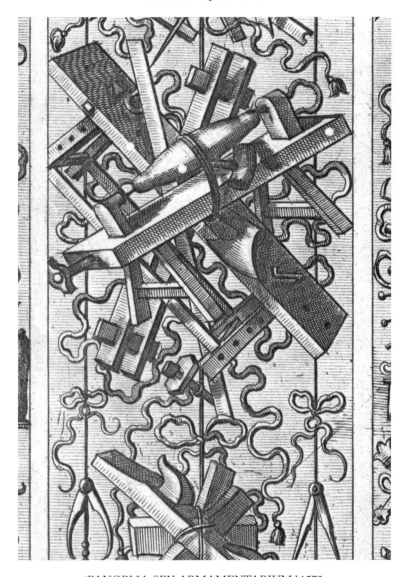

'PANOPLIA SEV ARMAMENTARIUM,' 1572
This engraving by Hans Vredeman de Vries shows a timber-framed bench behind the lathe.

A DRAWBORED MORTISE-&-TENON JOINT
This cutaway of a drawbored joint in ash shows how the oak peg has bent to pull the tenon into the mortise.

CHAPTER VI
JOINERY, LIKE A VOW

I'm eating a donut in Michigan while standing before the biggest pile of convenience-store pastries I have ever seen. I chew on one and stare at an older couple. They stare back, as the wife videotapes my every move. I chew; they film. I walk away; they follow.

This weirdness took place during two days at John Sindelar's workshop in southwest Michigan. Sindelar had a huge collection of antique and contemporary hand tools (he estimated it at "tens of thousands" of tools at its peak) and decided to open the collection to the public one weekend. I was there, as were my two new clingy friends.

Somewhere out there there's a videotape of this whole thing, but here's what happened and how it relates to workbenches.

In addition to owning acres of expensive old tools, Sindelar had also amassed the largest and most diverse collection of workbenches I've ever seen. The benches were strewn throughout the warehouse that housed his collection, and they were covered in antique tools.

I like old tools, but I adore old benches.

With my amateur film crew in tow I walked from workbench to workbench to examine the joinery, vises and accessories. Most of the benches were from the 19th and early 20th centuries, based on the vises and fasteners used on the benches.

What I learned that day transformed how I view workbench joinery, and…

But wait, the husband of the film crew (probably the key grip) has wandered away from his post to the bathroom, leaving me alone with the wife and the camera. I stare at her, and she lowers the camera.

"I hate your guts," she said in a low voice. "He (motioning to her husband) buys every single (expletive deleted) tool you've ever mentioned in the (expletive deleted) magazine and on the (expletive deleted) Internet. Thousands of dollars, and… (this speech goes on for a bit)."

I don't know what to say. What can you say? I decide to say some-

BENCH FROM THE SINDELAR COLLECTION
This unusual bench was assembled with drawbored mortise-and-tenon joints (the pegs are in the tool well).

thing, but I can see the husband is walking back now. The woman stops talking mid-sentence and raises the video camera back to her eye.

Anyway, what I learned about workbench joinery that day is that knockdown joinery can easily come loose. As I test-drove Sindelar's benches, I found a lot of them swayed. Their tusk tenons were loose. So I'd find a mallet (there were some solid gold ones lying about) and whack the tusks back in place, fixing the problem. I also found that the benches that relied on mechanical fasteners – especially lag screws or wood screws – had serious problems. The wood around these fasteners had been wallered out, and the fastener was holding on but not holding fast.

I began to think about all the benches I had made during the pre-

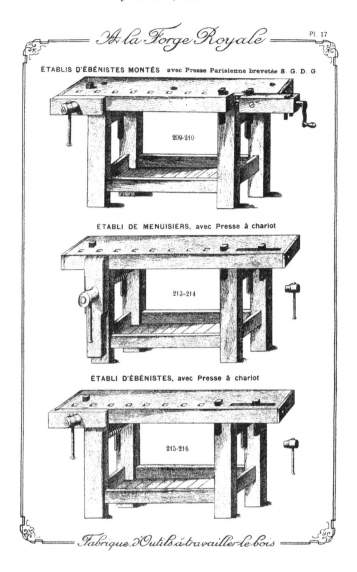

LA FORGE ROYALE CATALOG, 20TH CENTURY

These commercial benches from France used mortise-and-tenon joints for the base. The top is attached with wooden screws.

LA FORGE ROYALE BENCH
Despite its hard life, this workbench was still entirely sound.

vious years that incorporated lag bolts and wood screws. Were they doomed to fail?

Someone's videotape collection somewhere captured my internal struggle. I know I used the "faraway look in eyes" emotion, and I hope I win an award for my performance someday.

A few years later in Georgia I encountered a bench that finished the thought I began on donut day. Bo Childs, the guy who hosts the French Oak Roubo Project, had purchased a commercial French workbench made by La Forge Royale and imported it to Georgia.

The bench was likely from the early 20th century, based on the company's history and the bench's construction details. But what was important was how solid the bench remained, even though it had been beaten like a rented mule.

Some of the tenon shoulders had pulled away from their mortises (or the legs had shrunk). The benchtop was a mess of sawcuts and chisel marks. This bench had seen heaps of abuse at the hands of its French torturers. But it was still solid and ready to work.

That day is when I decided that the joint I prefer for a workbench is a pegged (preferably a drawbored) mortise-and-tenon joint. No lap joints, no tusks, no nuts, bolts and washers. While I am sure those forms of joinery can be engineered to work for the long term, why

JOINERY, LIKE A VOW

bother? There's already a joint that is perfect for the job. And it is the strongest and simplest of them all. The Lennie Small of joinery, if you will.

TELL ME ABOUT THE TENONS, GEORGE

For me, the joinery for a workbench is governed by two principles:

- If it can come loose, it will come loose.
- Simple, blind and massive is best.

The first principle is for people who wish to bolt their bench together. I used to be one of those people because I thought it would be an excellent way to knock down a workbench for travel.

Bench bolts with captured nuts are indeed a great way to build a knockdown workbench. And if you travel every month to a new city to set up your bench for a woodworking show, then this setup is a no-brainer. If you live on the fifth floor of a walk-up apartment without an elevator, a fall-to-pieces bench is the only answer. And if you build workbenches for customers, a knockdown workbench is far easier to ship.

For the rest of us, however, a knockdown workbench is more trouble and compromise than necessary. I think knockdown joinery should be the exception, not the rule.

The case in point for me is my $175 Workbench, which I first bolted together in 2000 and has not been unbolted since. It has lived in at least five buildings in three states. When we needed to move it, it was easier to throw it in a truck than take it apart. Unbolting a bench is a pain in the ass. You need a ratchet set. You need to keep track of the parts. And by the time you get it apart you could have thrown the whole bench into the back of a truck and been 45 minutes down the road. (An aside: A tusk-tenon bench is faster to knock down.)

When I tell people this fact, they contend that there is no disadvantage to having a knockdown bench. So why not add the bolts and nuts?

I have two arguments. First, installing a captured nut and bolt joint takes time, effort and jigging, especially the first time you attempt to install this kind of hardware. I've made many benches with this setup (plus many more beds), so I can attest that it's not Mensa-like difficult.

But the first time you do it, it is time-consuming. It requires accu-

THE ANARCHIST'S WORKBENCH

rate drilling with some shop-made jigs and a drill press. And if you screw it up and botch the location of the captured cross-nut, you are in for an afternoon of patching and re-drilling (been there). Making a simple mortise-and-tenon joint instead – without a captured nut – is faster, easier and less prone to error.

The second reason I eschew this joint (except when necessary) is a lesson I learned from teaching a class outside Atlanta, Ga.

After arriving at the school, they showed me the bench room, which was filled with heavy commercial workbenches. They were made with some sort of striped mahogany look-alike wood. That was odd. I'd never seen benches like this before (and haven't since).

While unpacking my tools, I leaned against one of the benches. It recoiled. That was weird. So, I grabbed its benchtop and found the whole bench swayed like a broken-down chair that hadn't quite given up the ghost. Alarmed, I gave a shake to the bench next to it. It also swayed.

All of the benches in the room ranged from full-on Festus from "Gunsmoke" to just a wee bit wobbly.

I scared up a ratchet set to tighten things up. But some of the bench bases wouldn't tighten up. The bolts had run out of threads, and the wood in the bases had become so compressed that things just couldn't be tightened. So, we had to get some washers to fill in the compressed areas. Eventually these workbench bases would become useless. Or they would have to be rebuilt.

Now, I'm sure that you could design a rock-hard bolt system that would outlast Western society. Those drunken workbenches at the school were on the downhill side of the bell curve of dumb design. But no matter what, you'll need to tighten your bolts every so often. We have a few benches that need a little help every winter when the plane totes and saw handles get loose because the humidity level has plummeted.

The same goes for tusk tenon joinery, a common early technique to build a workbench. I've built several Arts & Crafts bookcases using this joinery, and I've used many workbenches that feature it on the base. It is clever. It looks awesome. And it's incredibly strong when the tusks are hammered home hard.

But the simple act of working on the workbench can loosen up the tusks in my experience. And when winter comes, they are prone to

JOINERY, LIKE A VOW

BENCH BOLT HARDWARE
IF YOU REQUIRE A KNOCKDOWN BENCH, THIS HARDWARE IS IDEAL. BUT IT CAN COME LOOSE OVER TIME.

loosen. And the way they release their grip is slow and insidious, like turning up the heat gradually on a live lobster in a stove pot. You don't notice it until things are pretty bad. And by that time you have wasted a fair amount of energy working on a swaying workbench.

I have close friends who completely disagree with me on tusk tenons and say theirs never come loose. I believe them. It just hasn't been my experience.

For me, the bottom line is: If it can get loose, it will get loose.

One more note on bolts and other sorts of reversible joinery: Lag bolts (sometimes called lag screws) are not your fastening friend. I avoid them when attaching a benchtop to the workbench's base and when installing vises and other hardware (bolts plus washers and nuts are superior to lags). When properly installed, lags can last a long time. But if you over-tighten them, the lags can strip the wood surrounding the threads in a single rotation of the lag. Their grip is instantly ruined.

So, I avoid lag bolts as much as possible. And I avoid bolts and nuts

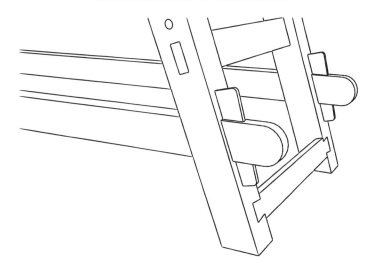

TUSK TENONS ON A WORKBENCH BASE
Tusk tenons, which are found on earlier benches that needed to be portable, can also come loose over time.

unless I absolutely positively need a knockdown bench. What's left? Simple wood-to-wood joinery.

SKIP THE FANCY BITS

The best joint for a workbench base is a well-fit mortise-and-tenon joint that is glued and drawbored. You can fuss over the dimensions and details of the joint (which we will do here in a bit) but know that if you put a thick tenon into a thick-walled mortise in a substantial-sized leg, your bench will join millions of other workbenches that have survived hundreds of years of hard use. Add a large drawbored peg through that tenon and the joint is as good as can be.

The above statement is like a marriage vow. It is a forsaking of all other alluring joinery. Don't be a cheater and try to sneak off with a half-lap joint. It's easy (to make) but will leave you broken in the end. Ditto for a screwed-together frame of 2x4s with a plywood skin. Yes, you'll have done the deed in just a weekend, but you'll pay for that weekend years on down the road. Dowels? You animal.

JOINERY, LIKE A VOW

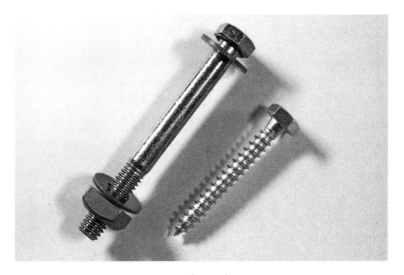

HEX-HEAD BOLT (LEFT) & LAG SCREW
Bolts can be tightened if they come loose. Lag screws can easily strip out the wood around them.

Another consideration is how the base attaches to the benchtop. I've already tried to ward you away from lag screws, which leaves us (again) with wood-on-wood joinery. Some benches use gravity and unglued dowels between the base and heavy top. This is my least favorite way to join the top and base. When you move the bench, the top can/will leap off. If you are building a knockdown workbench, this might be the best solution. But for a stay-put workbench, you can do better.

A fair number of the old French benches use a fancy joint that has a sliding dovetail and a through-tenon on the top of each leg. This joint pierces the benchtop and looks nice. It holds the base to the benchtop just fine.

And though I've put this joint on many, many workbenches (customers love it), it is not my favorite way to join the base to the benchtop. That's because for the first few years after you build the bench, the top continues to shrink, and the end grain of the tenon and dovetail become proud. Every few months it verges into annoying and you have to plane the end grain down so you can get back to work.

TENON & SLIDING DOVETAIL JOINT
AS THE BENCHTOP SHRINKS, THE END GRAIN OF THE LEGS BECOMES PROUD AND INTERFERES WITH SOME OPERATIONS UNTIL IT IS PLANED FLUSH.

This annoyance is worth it, however, because of the functional advantage of the through-joint. And that advantage is… well, actually there isn't one. After years of working on workbenches with this beautiful joint, I have found zero practical use for it. You might argue that it's a great end grain "anvil" for some operations, but that is a stretch.

The fancy French joint is straightforward to cut – nothing to fear. So, if you want to impress people and add some time to the construction process of your bench, feel free to add it. But don't fool yourself into thinking it's better.

So what's the best way to join the base and the benchtop? Just like when building the bench's base, I prefer a blind mortise and tenon that has been drawbored.

If you are a wood movement nerd, I am sure the above discussion has sparked a small stroke in your midbrain. Don't you have to allow the benchtop to expand and contract? No, you don't. The entire bench frame might become a little distorted as the top shrinks, but I've never seen one tear itself apart or become non-functioning. The proof is all

JOINERY, LIKE A VOW

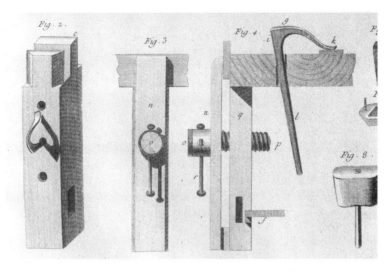

'L'ART DU MENUISIER,' PLATE 11 DETAIL
WHILE IT'S ONE OF THE PRETTIEST WORKBENCH JOINTS, IT OFFERS FEW
FUNCTIONAL ADVANTAGES COMPARED TO A BLIND MORTISE AND TENON.

around you if you look at old benches.

COMPONENT DIMENSIONS

Before we can talk about the dimensions of the joints, we have to talk about the dimensions of the parts of your workbench. Good workbench joinery begins with thick members. You are building an elephant, not a gazelle.

Most wooden parts for furniture projects are 1" to 2" thick, with some cabriole-shaped exceptions. When it comes to workbench components, you should think bigger – 5" thick isn't ridiculous for the legs or the benchtop. For the stretchers between the legs, I think 2" stock (or thicker if you have it) is just fine. The core strength of a good old-école workbench emanates from the joints between the benchtop and the legs. The stretchers are mostly along for the ride and to help make a shelf. So thinner stuff is acceptable for the stretchers, though I shoot for 2-1/2" thick when possible.

THE ANARCHIST'S WORKBENCH

JOINERY DIMENSIONS

There are lots of rules for making mortise-and-tenon joints. But the best rule is the oldest rule documented in the English language by Joseph Moxon in the 17th century. It is worth giving him the floor on this matter because there is nuance to consider.

> *You must take care in mortising and tenoning, that as near as you can equalize the strength of the sides of the mortise to the strength of the tenon. I do not mean that the stuff should be of an equal substance, for that is not equaling the strength. But the equaling strength must be considered with respect to the quality, position and substance of the stuff. If you were to make a tenon upon a piece of fir, and a mortise to receive it in a piece of oak, and the fir and oak have both the same size, the tenon therefore made upon this piece of fir must be considerably bigger than a tenon need be made of oak, because fir is a much weaker wood than oak, and therefore ought to have a greater substance to equal the strength of the oak. And for position, the shorter the stuff that the tenon is made on, the less violence the tenon is subject to. Besides, it is easier to split wood with the grain, than to break wood across the grain; and therefore the same wood when made as a tenon is stronger than the same wood of the same size when made as a mortise. For the injury a mortise is subject to is splitting with the grain of the wood, which without good care it will often do in working. But the force that must injure a tenon must offend it across the grain of the wood, in which position it will best endure violence.*
>
> *When two pieces of wood of the same quality and substance {as in this our example} are elected to make on the one a tenon and in the other mortise [the following is what you should consider]. If you make the mortise too wide, the sides of the mortise will be weaker than the sides that contain the mortise. And if one be weaker than the other, the weakest will give way to the strongest when an equal violence is offered to both. Therefore you may see a necessity of equalizing the strength of one to the other as near you can. But because no rule is extant to do it by, nor can {for many considerations I think} a rule be made, therefore this equalizing of strength must be referred to the judgment of the operator. Now to the work.*

JOINERY, LIKE A VOW

DISTORTED WORKBENCH BASE

The benchtop on this workbench shrank, pulling the undercarriage into an A shape. The bench remains sound and functional.

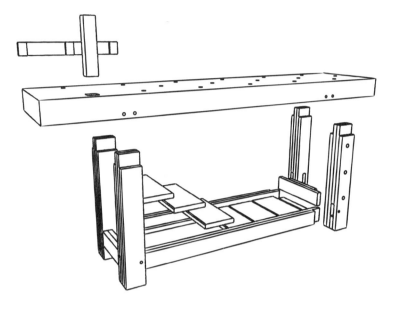

ANARCHIST'S WORKBENCH, EXPLODED VIEW
All the joints are blind and drawbored mortise and tenons.

Translation: The best rule is experience. My addendum: If you don't have experience, just overbuild the whole thing and you'll be fine.

Here's how I work through the process of designing a typical workbench's joints. Let's say the benchtop is 5" thick and the legs are 5" thick. The stretchers are 2-1/2" thick. To join the legs to the benchtop, everything is so thick that I can fall on an old rule that says the tenon should be one-half the thickness of the tenoned member. The leg is 5" thick, so the tenon can be 2-1/2" thick. That is massive.

If I center the tenon on the leg, then both the mortise wall in the benchtop and the shoulder of the tenon will be 1-1/4" thick. That is substantial and would be acceptable on a timber-framed building.

Now let's look at the stretchers down below for the base. They are 2-1/2" thick. If I make the tenon half that thickness (1-1/4") and center the tenon on the stretcher, then the mortise wall (and tenon shoulder) will be 5/8". That seems skimpy in comparison to the other joints

JOINERY, LIKE A VOW

in the bench. Is that too weak? Maybe. Maybe not. But why take a chance?

My recommendation is to use a "bare face" tenon. Make the tenon 1-1/4" thick with a 1-1/4" shoulder on only one side (the outside) and no shoulder at the inside (that's its "bare face"). This arrangement offers a massive 1-1/4" shoulder at the outside of the leg-to-stretcher joint. And any minor gaps from the lack of a shoulder at the back are concealed by a shelf. Or by the fact that no one looks back there anyway.

This is how I keep Moxon in mind and balance the strength of both the tenon and the mortise walls.

Everything written above is about the thickness of the tenons. What about the lengths? Make the tenons as long as is practical. For the stretchers down below, the length of their tenons depends on how you arrange the stretchers. If the four stretchers are all the same distance from the floor, then the tenons can only be so long before they collide with a tenon from a neighboring stretcher. If the stretchers are different distances from the floor, the tenons can pass all the way through the legs. Either arrangement is fine.

For the tenons poking into the benchtop, I think you should leave enough wood above the tenons to allow the benchtop to be flattened many times without encountering the tenons.

With a 5"-thick benchtop, 3"-long tenons on the legs will give me 2" of wood to flatten away during my lifetime and the lifetimes of future generations.

DRAWBORING

Drawboring a mortise-and-tenon joint adds a mechanical lock to what is already an excellent joint. You take a peg and drive it through holes in both the mortise and the tenon. But here's the trick: The hole in the tenon is offset just a little toward the tenon's shoulder (I use a 1/8" offset in bench building). Driving in a stout peg tries to pull the holes into alignment – some might say it draws the bores in line. But what it really does is bend the peg.

Once again, this technique is a balancing act. A too-skinny peg will split when driven in. A too-thick peg will wreck the tenon, usually popping the end off the tenon and making the peg useless.

For bench building, I like a 5/8"-diameter oak peg with dead-

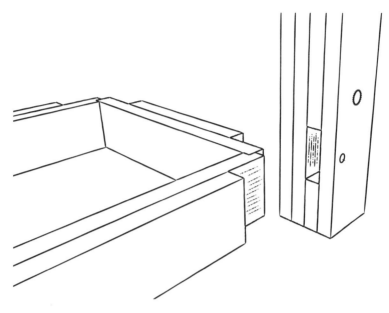

BAREFACE TENONS
Here you can see how the tenons intersect inside the leg. They can be joined with a miter or a rabbet (shown).

straight grain. I've experimented with bigger and smaller pegs, and I seem to have the best results with 5/8". My second-favorite size is 3/4".

Where should the peg be located through the tenon? Good question. I divide the tenon into thirds. If the tenon is 3" long, the hole should be about 1" away from the shoulder of the tenon. More details on the act of drawboring for workbenches are located in the chapters on constructing the workbench.

AVOID THE ROAD TO RUIN

In my past, I built many workbenches that use metal fasteners as a way to simplify construction. I'm not alone, of course. Many magazines (and videos) tout how you can build their workbench design in a day or a weekend. The words "fast, easy and cheap" sell magazines and generate clicks.

JOINERY, LIKE A VOW

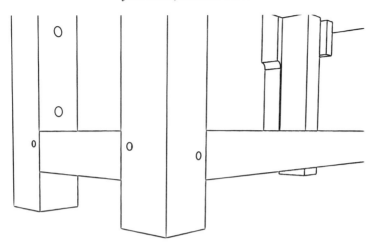

STRETCHERS IN-LINE, WORKBENCH BASE
With stretchers all the same distance from the floor, you will need to use blind mortises.

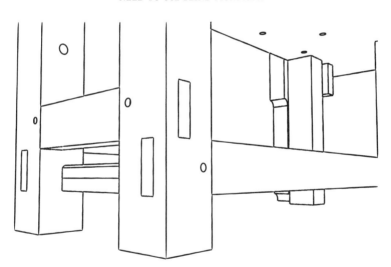

OFFSET STRETCHERS, WORKBENCH BASE
By changing the location of the end stretchers you can use through-tenons.

THE ANARCHIST'S WORKBENCH

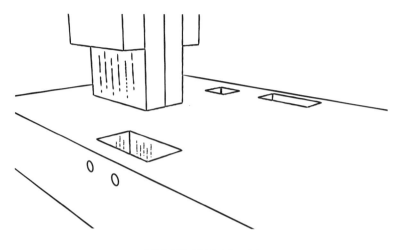

LEG-TO-TOP JOINT
A BLIND MORTISE-AND-TENON JOINT MEANS THE END GRAIN FROM THE LEG WILL NOT INTERFERE WITH THE BENCHTOP.

Shortcuts in workbench joinery are a dangerous gimmick, just like the restaurant by my old office that sold half-price sushi. Nothing involving cheap joinery or dodgy fish has a happy ending.

The archaeological record proves this point: The workbenches that have survived were built with simple mortise-and-tenon joints. I've seen 200-year-old benches that are as solid as the day they were made. And I've seen plywood benches from the 1970s that couldn't hold a houseplant.

To sum up my joinery advice: Don't screw yourself.

JOINERY, LIKE A VOW

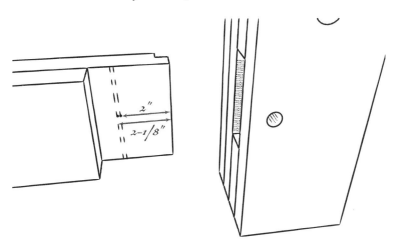

DRAWBORE DETAIL
The hole through the tenon is offset 1/8" toward the shoulder of the tenon. This provides the mechanical interlock.

WORKBENCH IN THE WHITE, 2005
MY FIRST FRENCH YELLOW-PINE WORKBENCH. WHILE SIMILAR TO THE BENCH IN THIS BOOK, THE NEW BENCH HAS IMPROVED WORKHOLDING AND A THICKER TOP.

CHAPTER VII
MAKE IT DAMN BIG (MOSTLY)

The biggest mental hurdle to building my first French workbench in 2005 was the size of the bench and its components.

I had translated A.J. Roubo's paragraphs on workbenches from "l'Art du menuisier," and they had me perplexed. The bench should be as much as 12' long. The top is 5" to 6" thick and 20" to 22" wide. The legs are 4" thick x 6" wide. The stretchers are 2" x 4".

This isn't a bench. It's a house for a wee French person.

Where was I going to get wood that size? And how could I pay for it? I didn't have much money; Lucy and I were still paying blood ransom to day care (the kids were 9 and 4). So I knew I was going to have to rely on an old friend, yellow pine.

Then there was the problem of finding the time to build it (the kids were 9 and 4) without stranding poor Lucy (the kids were 9 and 4).

Bright idea: Build the bench for the magazine. At the time we were publishing two woodworking magazines, *Popular Woodworking* and a new publication called *Woodworking Magazine* (for which the staff wrote every word), so there was an enormous black hole that had to be filled with words, photos and drawings every month.

At the time we were getting *Woodworking Magazine* (god rest its soul) up and running and were agonizing over the projects for the autumn 2005 issue. On the night before our editorial meeting to decide on the projects, I drafted the Roubo workbench in yellow pine.

This, I thought, should be the cover project.

I finished the proposal hours after my family had gone to bed. I slept for a couple hours then headed to the editorial meeting at our graphic designer's house. I passed out construction drawings of the bench to everyone and took a deep breath.

You probably know how this ends.

I blurted: "I'll pay for the wood. It won't cost the magazine a thing."

Steve: "Sold."

I started building it the next day.

THE ANARCHIST'S WORKBENCH

The glue was barely dry on that bench, and I was still puzzling over where to put the holdfast holes (an internal debate that took 15 years to settle) when Deneb Puchalski at Lie-Nielsen Toolworks asked to borrow it.

He was traveling to the Cincinnati area for a show for Woodcraft's suppliers and needed a bench for demonstrations.

It's hard to say no to Deneb – he's a good friend – so I managed to get the monster bench to the loading dock of the Northern Kentucky Convention Center and onto a rolling cart. As I wheeled the bench past the show's other vendors, people stared.

"Now that's a bench," one guy called from his booth.

It was the closest I'll ever hear to a wolf whistle. Then a guy blocked my path.

"Did you build this?" he asked. "I'd like to buy it. How much?"

"I don't even know if it works," I said. "It's an experiment." He gave me his business card and told me to call him.

This was the first glimmer that this bench design was going to be more than a footnote in my life. At the least, people liked the way it looked. And compared to all the other benches on the convention floor that day, it looked like a monster – 8' long with elephantine components. The top was 4" x 24" x 96". The legs were a tree-trunky 5" x 5". The stretchers were 2-1/2" x 3".

Every aspect of every workbench design, from the wood to the vises, elicits scrutiny and division in the woodworking field. But nothing foments more arguments than the overall dimensions of a workbench. Which has always struck me as amusing because that's like fighting over which shirt size is the best ever – I'm a 16/34, and I will fight you.

Here we go.

Your bench should be sized to suit your workshop, your work and you. I think the size of your workbench is like the size of a good meal. Too little is frustrating and never enough. Too much might seem like heaven at first but might create some long-term problems.

BENCHTOP LENGTH

Mostly, the length of your bench should be dictated first by how far apart the walls of your shop are. You need some open space at each end of the bench for you to stand and do stuff. And you need some airspace if you use handplanes. No one wants to chuck a plane through the drywall.

MAKE IT DAMN BIG (MOSTLY)

FRENCH WORKBENCHES
THE INSPIRATION FOR THIS WORKBENCH'S CHUNKY LEG VISE CAME DIRECTLY FROM THIS POSTCARD.

Shoot for 36" of airspace at either end of the bench. Or, in a pinch, 36" at the one end of the bench where you work the most. The space that's left is a decent dimension for the length of your benchtop.

What if you have a huge shop – 20' x 20'? Should your bench be 14' long? Well it can be, but it won't be fun to move your bench (and I promise that you will move your bench quite a lot). In theory, a long bench is great. You can work long mouldings on it. And you can cut joinery at one end of the bench with parts stacked at the other.

For general furniture construction – cabinets, chairs, shelves and the like – I like a bench that is somewhere between 7' and 9' long. Most of my benches end up about 8' long (or a few inches shorter) because that is ideal for building it with 8'-long lumber. Buying 12'-long sticks for a 9'- or 10'-long workbench can be wasteful.

So, I gather the best lumber I can find for the benchtop. I trim off minor end-checks. And that's the bench's length. It's not scientific.

To be honest, I can't tell you how long my current oak workbench is without consulting a tape measure. It's about 8'. Or, as I like to tell

THE ANARCHIST'S WORKBENCH

DOMINY WORKBENCH, WINTERTHUR MUSEUM
One of the longest extant workbenches I've seen, the Dominy family bench was used for a wide variety of furniture-making tasks.

my wife, it's long enough. (I just checked it and [my bench] is 95-3/8".)

In the course of teaching hundreds of people to build benches at schools, I've had a few students experience a near-mental meltdown because their shop is a spare apartment bedroom that can handle only a 5' or 6' bench. Once again, I think this is where yellow pine shines. Make your shorty bench out of yellow pine with nice vises; do the best job you can. If/when you are blessed by the pole barn fairy, then remove the bench's vises and build a bigger yellow pine bench for your new space. You'll be out less than $200, and you can sell (or give away) the old bench's bones to another apartment dweller.

BENCHTOP WIDTH

The width of a bench is another case where having too much can bite the hinder. I like a bench that's about 24" wide – a tad less is fine. That width makes it easy to move the bench through doorways, up stairs and around normal hallway corners (even with the vises attached).

MAKE IT DAMN BIG (MOSTLY)

And it's plenty wide for making furniture. You can get all four legs of a typical chair sitting flat on the benchtop. A typical 20"-wide cabinet side fits perfectly there for planing. You can sleeve typical drawers with 42"-long fronts over the end of the bench to plane them up. And if your tools are in a rack at the back or on the wall, you can easily reach across to grab them.

There's a reason that this width has been standard for hundreds of years in Western workshops.

What about a narrower bench? I've made them as narrow as 18-1/2" wide. These are a bit tippy when you are traversing panels with a jack plane (I brace these benches against a wall or another workbench). You can't get all four legs of an assembled chair perched on the benchtop. And typical 20"-wide panels have to be shifted laterally a bit so you can plane them up. It works – it's just a little awkward.

(Side note: If you inherit a too-narrow workbench, it's not a crime to laminate more planks to the back edge of the benchtop. Yeah, the wood will look different. But it's a bench, not a tea table.)

What about a wider bench – 36" or 48" wide? Yes, these exist. I've worked on them. Yes, they are nice for a few operations where you need acres of space, such as stacking all the parts for 12 full-size tool chests.

Wide benches are, in my experience, mostly a pain. Moving them is no fun unless you work in a garage or warehouse. Reaching across the bench to get a tool that's rolled 40" away is inconvenient. But mostly, I dislike them because they take up valuable floor space – square footage I could use for sawbenches, a band saw or a lathe. In a pinch, I say you can stack your million furniture parts on sawbenches or the impressive floor space you saved by having a normal-sized workbench.

TOOL TRAYS & BENCHTOP WIDTH

Sadly, we've come to the part of the book where we talk about tool trays. I think they're a plot by bench manufacturers (or designers) to cheat you of usable benchtop space. Having a solid 14"-wide benchtop with a 10"-wide tool tray is nothing like having a 24"-wide benchtop. It's like having a 14"-wide benchtop with a 10"-wide compost bin attached to it.

Some people "solve" this problem by covering the tool tray with a removable panel. And voilà, they have the best of both worlds – a hamster habitat hidden below and a wide, uninterrupted benchtop. Except you can't use holdfasts back there. And you can't store anything in the tool tray because it will become mostly inaccessible while you are working.

For students who insist on a tool tray, I offer this solution. Make the benchtop a 24"-wide slab then add a tool tray on the back of the bench that hangs on a French cleat. You can remove the tray in a moment if you need the back of your bench accessible for some weird clamping operation. And you haven't given up any valuable benchtop space.

The only downside to my suggestion is that you have to stretch to get your tools in the tray.

Lervad, a Danish workbench manufacturer, has additional solutions you can swipe. The company makes a tool tray that is removable and is not the full length of the benchtop. It can be installed at the rear of the benchtop up by the face vise. Or it can be installed on the left end of the benchtop. If it were me, however, I'd put the tray at the other end of the benchtop. When I plane a board, the shavings go right off the end of the benchtop and into the garbage can. So I don't want a tool tray there.

BENCH HEIGHT

Here's a tip on self-care: Decline to argue about workbench height. The only person who can answer the question is you. You have to think about your work and your tools. For example, if you prefer metal bench planes instead of wooden bench planes, a taller bench might be in order. Wooden planes hold your hands about 3" off the benchtop. Metal planes hold your hands about 1/4" off the benchtop.

Plus remember: Your bench can be raised or lowered in the future if you choose poorly. And, there isn't one ideal height for a person. It's more like a range of about 3" where things feel good, better or best.

Also, you can build accessories to improve the ergonomics of common operations. Build a Moxon vise for dovetailing so you don't have to stoop over. Build an "etaux" (aka a Benchcrafted HiVise) for planing legs or spindles. Build a small tabletop bench that stacks on your regular benchtop if you need your face right up against your electric router.

Historically, I have found that most workbenches range from about 28" to 36" high. A too-tall workbench is nice for close operations such

MAKE IT DAMN BIG (MOSTLY)

LERVAD WORKBENCH, 20TH CENTURY
THIS DANISH WORKBENCH FEATURES AN UNUSUAL TOOL TRAY. THE COMPANY ALSO MAKES A VERSION WHERE THE TRAY IS ON THE END OF THE BENCHTOP.

MOXON VISE, ALSO CALLED A DOUBLE-SCREW VISE
LOW WORKBENCHES ARE IDEAL FOR PLANING OPERATIONS. IF YOU NEED TO
RAISE YOUR WORK FOR DOVETAILING, A BENCHTOP VISE IS IDEAL.

as carving, but exhausting for general operations (planing, especially). Lower benches encourage me to use my torso when planing. Taller benches conscript my arms to do the work.

A few modern makers insist on benches taller than the historical norm. They say it's a health issue – taller benches save your back. I have not found this to be true with normal people with normal backbones. But you might be an exception – I can't say.

When I encounter an operation that requires me to be close to the work – chopping dovetail waste, mortising, carving, in-your-face detail work – I sit my butt down. I sit as much as possible both to conserve energy and get my eyes close to the work. Or I use a Moxon vise, an étaux or I grab the object with handscrews in my face vise.

So, with all that preamble, how do I determine how high my workbench should be inside the historical range of 28" to 36"? I stand with my arms relaxed by my side and measure from the floor to the point where my pinky finger joins my hand. That's my personal ideal.

MAKE IT DAMN BIG (MOSTLY)

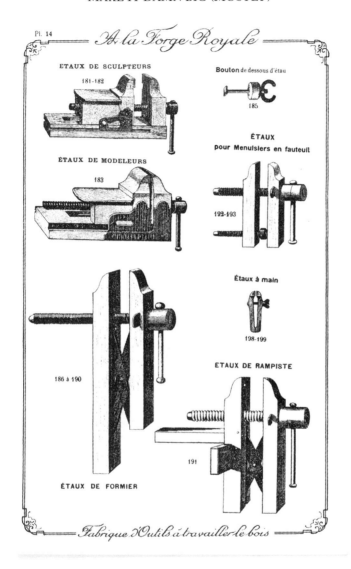

LA FORGE ROYALE CATALOG, 20ᵀᴴ CENTURY
A VARIETY OF VISES DESIGNED TO RAISE THE WORK OFF THE BENCHTOP.

THE ANARCHIST'S WORKBENCH

When I measure other woodworkers (at their insistence), I might add 1" to that measurement, which they can remove later from the bottom of the legs with a handsaw. If my measurement falls outside of the historical range, I step back and take a look at the person. Are they ridiculously tall or short? Is their torso long like a grasshopper? Do they have stumpy wiener-dog legs?

Even with these people I usually shift their purported bench height toward the historical norm a bit. If there's time, I have them work on some workbenches of different heights to see how they fare.

And if all else fails, I recommend something a little taller because that's an easy fix with a saw (especially with the French/Wierix workbench design compared to a sled-foot workbench base).

By the way, I'm 6'3". My inseam is 34". I'm a Gemini. And I prefer a 34"-high workbench.

The size of a workbench is something that has been carefully considered for centuries. It relates to the human body and the built world around it. Fooling around with those dimensions can result in a real snakebite. Think carefully before wandering from the main trail.

DIVORCE IS HARD ON WORKBENCHES

Here's my last bit on the importance of historical workbench sizes. Whenever I mention how important it is to be able to move a workbench across town or across the country, most woodworkers respond: "Bah, I'm never moving." And so, they build a subterranean monstrosity that will never emerge in one piece.

Then life grinds their gears.

My business partner, John Hoffman, ran headfirst into this problem with a workbench I made (so the design flaw was all mine). He inherited the Nicholson workbench I'd built in 2006 for the "Workbenches" book, and it lived against the wall in his basement workshop.

He then renovated his basement – he improved the stairwell and the overall look of the place. Shortly thereafter, he and his wife separated, and the bench had to vacate the basement.

For some reason, I'd built that bench with a 27"-wide top (wider than usual), 34" high and 96" long. That sucker would not make the turn around the corner of the renovated stairwell.

It was a game of inches. And in the end, the stairwell and the bench both ended up with significant scars. John had to patch the drywall,

A BIG BENCH; SMALL DEAL

A few months after walking my yellow pine Roubo through the local convention center, I was so smitten with the thing that I decided to write a book about ancient workbenches. I was spending my free time researching old workbench designs in tool catalogs, woodworking books and fine art paintings.

My plan was to make the book the same way my college band used to make music – punk DIY style. I was going to write, edit and design the book. Then publish it on my own time on a photocopier. Maybe I could sell the "book" to students at woodworking schools where I taught. Make some beer money. That way I wouldn't have to worry if it was an embarrassment, or even ask permission from my employer. Because really: Who would want to read a book about ancient workbenches? At the time I couldn't even imagine pitching my idea to the company's book division, which printed a regular cycle of router book, router book, table saw, carved Santa.

I wrote the book during nights and weekends, both in Kentucky and while on the road for the magazine. About halfway through the writing process, I took a trip to Maine for the 25th anniversary of Lie-Nielsen Toolworks with my friend (and now business partner) John.

I had brought along a box of Esther Price chocolates to give to Tom Lie-Nielsen's wife, Karyn, but they had completely melted into a single brown blob during my journey. So, after the celebration, John and I got roaring drunk in our cabin and ate the entire blob, smudging our faces and hands. Painted in milk chocolate, I unloaded all my worries about the workbench book on John. Was it going to suck?

John said (and I'll clean up the language in case you are reading this book to your kids at bedtime), "I was talking to Christian Becksvoort today and asked him why he hadn't written any more books after 'Shaker Legacy.' Becksvoort said there was no money in woodworking books."

Somehow, we came up with the idea to start a publishing company that didn't screw authors. We decided we could start by selling my "Workbenches" book on the Internet (no matter who was the publisher). Then maybe we could publish other unpublishable books. Or something. I forget.

It was all just late-night, beer-fueled "you-know-what-we-should-do?" stuff.

The next morning, we were hungover as we headed to the Portland, Maine, airport. But we remembered the gist of the drunken conversation. While waiting for my flight at the airport's gate I began writing an outline of a fair publishing contract, and I drew up the structure of a publishing company we named Lost Art Press.

This is where my corporate training/loathing came in handy. As I wrote the hippie-fied contract, I simply scratched in the opposite of what I had learned to do in corporate publishing.

Instead of paying the authors about 15 percent royalties, we thought we could split all expenses and profits 50/50. Instead of specifying that we had complete control over the manufacturing, editing and title of each book, we could make all those decisions with the help of the author; everyone had to be happy before a book went to press.

I closed my laptop and got on the airplane to go home. It was a nice idea, but maybe a little too heavy a dose of rainbows and Smurfs.

NOBODY DOES THAT

I finished writing, editing and designing "Workbenches: From Design & Theory to Construction & Use" during the summer of 2007. It was ready to go to the photocopier (or to the fire pit in my backyard). But first I had to jump through a flaming administrative hoop.

F+W Media, the now-defunct company that owned *Popular Woodworking* and *Woodworking Magazine*, required its employees to submit any book manuscripts for a "first right of refusal." I printed out my book and handed it over to one of the book editors in his cubicle. He said he'd look it over and get back to me in a couple weeks.

In less than an hour, my phone rang. They wanted to publish the book.

On the one hand, I was elated that someone thought it was good enough to publish. But then came the contract negotiations.

"When it comes to books by F+W employees, we can't offer you royalties. We can offer you a flat fee of $10,000," the editor said.

Hmm, I thought, two years of work for $10,000? That seemed… skimpy.

I asked, "So, there's no negotiating room?"

MAKE IT DAMN BIG (MOSTLY)

"Well, you can refuse the offer," he said. "But nobody does that."

Translation: In the polite-on-the-surface world of mid-sized Midwest publishers, the words "nobody does that" is the equivalent of finding a bloody horse head in your waterbed.

I needed to keep my magazine job. In fact, I was deeply grateful for my job. I still consider it the best job I ever had. So, I agreed to the terms. On the upside, F+W agreed to print the book in the United States, which seemed a victory until I realized I hadn't gotten that in writing. So, they weren't bound by it.

F+W's book division went to work and released the book in the fall of 2007.

Pretty much I did everything wrong with my negotiations, and F+W did everything right. Hat tip to them for the lesson in corporate publishing.

But there was a bright side. One of the clauses in my F+W contract encouraged me to start a website and sell the book myself. There was no marketing budget for my title, so it was my job to both write the book and help push it.

So, John and I decided to incorporate Lost Art Press as a limited liability corporation in Kentucky. We'd sell the "Workbenches" book to make some beer money. Maybe we could also sell T-shirts or some reprints of old woodworking books.

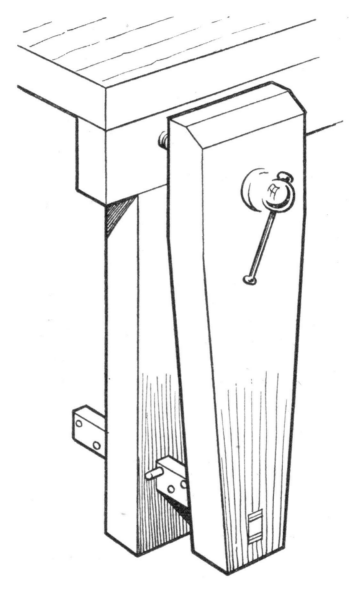

LEG VISE, UNITED KINGDOM, 20TH CENTURY
THE CLASSIC LEG VISE FORM WITH A PARALLEL GUIDE. NOTE HOW HIGH THE SCREW IS DRAWN IN THIS EXAMPLE.

CHAPTER VIII
WORKHOLDING: EDGES & ENDS

Growing up in a quick-release vise society, I had doubts about how well a leg vise would work. I had seen hundreds of images of them as I researched ancient benches, but I had never worked with one until I built one.

I can still remember the giant creak the mechanism made as I cinched it down on a scrap for the first time. I then grabbed the scrap and tried to yank it loose (unsuccessfully). That was a good day.

To be sure, I understood the theory of how it worked in conjunction with a parallel guide at the floor (and later, a Crisscross mechanism), but I didn't know how effective the vise would be. Would it wobble laterally without parallel-guide bars? (Yes, but that allows it to hold tapered workpieces.) Would it hold work as firmly as an iron-jawed screw vise? (Yes.) Would I get annoyed at moving the pin in the parallel guide to accommodate different thicknesses of work? (Yes, but not as much as I suspected.)

In other words, I was like every other workbench builder who contemplates a vise he or she has never used – or even seen in person. You can grasp the theory, but how well does it really work? Is it lame? Weak? Inconvenient? Fussy? Did you just flush $200 dollars into a piece of equipment that will mock you every time you step up to the bench?

Maybe….

The following vises are what I consider mainstream designs. These are vises that have been around for a long time and have proven reliable.

When you encounter vises that are outside of the following list, that doesn't mean you should automatically avoid them. You just need to know that you are a laboratory rat – who volunteered. And that's fine. Some people love to download beta software to their computers. Others are still using MS-DOS on 5-1/4" floppy discs to run their missile silos.

LEG VISE WITHOUT A PARALLEL GUIDE
SOME EARLY LEG VISES ARE SHOWN WITHOUT A PARALLEL GUIDE. THE OPPOSING FORCE IS SUPPLIED BY A SCRAP OF WOOD OR (IN THIS CASE) THE FLOOR.

WORKHOLDING: EDGES & ENDS

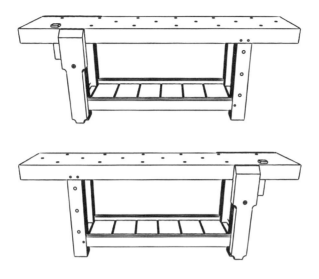

RIGHT- AND LEFT-HANDED WORKBENCHES
The face vise is positioned on the left leg of the bench for right-handers. And on the other end for left-handers.

First let's get a few basic terms out of the way so we're all speaking the same language.

WHAT'S A FACE VISE?

The face vise is on the front of your workbench. If you're right-handed, it goes on the left-hand side of the benchtop. If you're left-handed, it goes on the right. Why? Usually when planing long boards, it's more comfortable to plane from right to left if you are right-handed (and the opposite way when you are a lefty).

It's better to plane toward the vise screw, rather than away from it. This is from the days when vises didn't have parallel bars. By planing toward the screw, the board gets tighter in the vise's jaws. If you plane away from the vise screw, the racked jaw can spit out the board like a watermelon seed between your fingers. Yes, I've had this happen.

Face vises are almost all driven by screws, either wood or metal.

DOUBLE- & SINGLE-START SCREWS
A DOUBLE-START SCREW (LEFT) HAS TWO INDEPENDENT THREADS AND MOVES TWICE AS FAST AS A SINGLE-START SCREW (RIGHT).

The screws for woodworking are typically single-start or double-start. A single-lead start has one continuous thread cut into the shaft of the screw and is simplest to manufacture. The distance between the teeth of the screw is called the "pitch." The amount the jaw of your vise travels with one full rotation of the screw is called the "lead." With a single-start screw, the pitch and the lead are the same.

For example: The pitch of my face-vise screw is 5/8" from gullet to gullet. When I rotate the screw 360°, the vise's jaw moves 5/8".

A double-start screw has two independent threads cut into the shaft. The lead is double the pitch. So if my vise had a double-start thread with a 5/8" pitch it would move the jaw 1-1/4" with every full rotation.

In general, I prefer double-start screws. They are more expensive, but the jaw opens and closes faster.

The other anatomy in a face vise is the parallel bars. These run par-

WORKHOLDING: EDGES & ENDS

PARALLEL BARS, QUICK-RELEASE VISE
The steel tubes to either side of the screw help the jaw move smoothly. The bolts on the ends of the bars need to be almost snug to work correctly.

TYPICAL PARALLEL GUIDE

THE STEEL PIN IS MOVED TO DIFFERENT HOLES DEPENDING ON THE SIZE OF THE PIECE BEING CLAMPED IN THE JAW ABOVE.

allel to the vise's screw and prevent the jaw from racking too badly when you clamp a tapered or irregular workpiece. They also assist you in moving the jaw of a quick-release vise open or closed. With these vises, when you engage the quick-release mechanism, the screw drops out of the mechanism temporarily and the jaw slides open or shut on the parallel bars. Not all vises have them or need them, however.

A somewhat similar internal organ with some face vises is what's called the "parallel guide." Like the parallel bars, a parallel guide slides in and out with the jaw. But its job is mostly to provide a pivot point on which to close the jaws. The jaw will screw freely in and out until a movable pin in the parallel guide encounters the leg of the bench. Then the jaw pivots and clamps – hard – whatever is between the jaws of the vise.

The remainder of the anatomy is simple. The jaw is the movable clamping surface of the vise. The "tommy bar" is what helps you rotate

NOTCH IN A SHAKER WORKBENCH, OHIO COLONY
Notches show up in benchtops across centuries and cultures. A workpiece (or appliance) can be wedged in place in the notch.

the screw easily, and it adds leverage when needed. The "hub" is the unthreaded end of the screw that the tommy bar passes through.

Now that you know all the parts, we should ask if you even need a face vise. Well, you need something, but it doesn't have to be a screw-driven vise that you add to the bench. It could be something that you have taken away from the bench.

NOTCHES

While researching early workbenches, I found several examples of paintings and drawings that showed a simple square or rectangular notch sawn into the edge of the benchtop – sometimes on the end of the bench; sometimes on the front edge.

The notch allows you to hold work immobile with the addition of a wedge. I have had the best luck with softwood wedges with a shallow pitch – only a degree or two. You pound the wedge between the work

SAWING A TENON USING A NOTCH
SOFTWOOD WEDGES PROVIDE EXCELLENT HOLDING POWER.

WORKHOLDING: EDGES & ENDS

INSTALLING A CROCHET, 2005
THIS SIMPLE WOODEN HOOK CAN HELP HOLD YOUR WORK WHEN PLANING THE LONG EDGES OF BOARDS.

and the notch, and you are woodworking. It works incredibly well and is the cheapest and simplest face vise imaginable.

The notch has significant limitations, however. It's best for working on narrow bits – such as cutting tenon cheeks on a door's rail. You can use it for dovetailing by rotating the board 90°, but this technique has its limits in my experience. The unsupported edge of the board vibrates. And you need a selection of wedges to accommodate different thicknesses and widths of work.

But it doesn't cost anything other than your time. I have also used the notch when cutting scrollwork with a coping saw. The notch supports the work (flat on the bench) while I hold the saw vertical. And I'm certain there are other as-yet-undiscovered uses for the notch.

CROCHET

Working up the evolutionary ladder of face vises, the next step is the "crochet" or hook – a common accessory on early workbenches all over

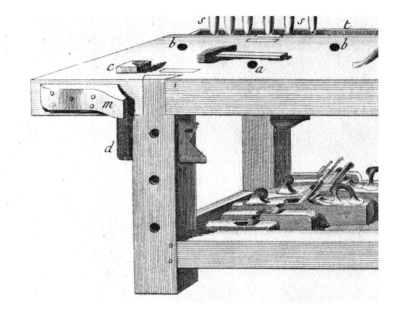

CROCHET, DETAIL FROM 'L'ART DU MENUISIER'
Many crochets have an opening that does not pinch the work, as shown here.

the West.

The hook is like an open bird's mouth mounted to the front edge of the benchtop. You shove the work in there, and the V-shaped opening restrains the work. You usually have to add something else to complete the workholding – a holdfast, a clamp or maybe just a couple pegs when planing the long edge of a board.

The crochet excels when planing the edges of long boards. If you have a lot of edge planing to do, use holdfasts to secure a 2x4 between the bench's legs to act as a platform for your work. Place your work on the 2x4 and plane away.

It's less effective for tenoning and dovetailing the ends of boards. You need to add something to the setup to get things working smoothly.

The openings of crochets tend to have either a shallow angle or basically no angle. For the latter kind, they work basically like a planing

WORKHOLDING: EDGES & ENDS

JOSEPH MOXON'S BENCH SCREW
MOXON ILLUSTRATED A CROCHET THAT WAS PIERCED WITH A SINGLE SCREW
FOR GRIPPING THE WORK, SIMILAR TO WHAT IS SHOWN HERE.

stop that has been positioned on the front face of the bench instead of on its benchtop.

I like using a crochet, but other vises are more convenient. Still, it requires only a chunk of wood plus a couple heavy nails or bolts to make. So, if you are poor or like working using old ways, it's an effective tool with a long history.

JOSEPH MOXON'S 'BENCH SCREW'

Take a crochet and add a single wooden vise screw to it. The wedged shape of the crochet holds one edge of the work against the front edge of the benchtop. The screw holds the work inside the crochet.

This improvement was discussed by Joseph Moxon in his 17th-century pamphlet "The Art of Joinery," which became part of his "Mechanick Exercises" book. He calls it the "bench screw." I built a version

SHOULDER VISE

THE SHOULDER VISE FEATURES A MOVABLE JAW THAT IS PROPELLED BY A SCREW.

into my crochet. It had a wooden screw with an octagonal handle.

It works and is an inexpensive vise to make if you have a threadbox and tap. But I have some cautions. First, the tip of the wooden screw tends to mar softwood workpieces. You can engineer some workarounds for this problem (inserting a scrap between the work and screw, adding a rotating pressure plate to the end of the screw etc.).

Second, the handle of the vise takes some getting used to. I wasn't thrilled about having a narrow handle protruding 6" to 10" from the bench in the same airspace as my soft bits. I indeed caught myself on it pretty good several times, so I removed the screw from the crochet when it wasn't in use.

SHOULDER VISE

The shoulder vise, which was popular on many 20th-century European workbenches, represents the continued evolution of the crochet and bench screw combination. This is its fully evolved form. The crochet is large – big enough to get an assembled drawer into. The screw has a sliding pressure plate. And the whole contraption (usually) requires an additional leg in the bench's base to keep everything stable.

I have used this vise – at woodworking shows, woodworking schools and in private workshops. But I have never owned a bench with this vise, so my criticism is from a skeptic at (literal) arm's length.

On the plus side, the vise offers a great way to clamp drawer sides for dovetailing. It holds tapered objects easily and is nice for edge planing. It can hold drawers and the like for cleaning them up, as well.

The downsides are noteworthy. The vise takes up enough space in front of the bench (11" is typical) that I feel like I have to reach over the vise to get to the work. It's almost an awkward movement for me. Aside from that, the vise adds a lot of complexity to the construction of the bench.

People I respect think it's the end-all vise for dovetailing. In my experience, it's not. I much prefer a Moxon vise that raises the work and allows me to get up close to it with ease.

LEG VISE

In the 19th and early 20th centuries, leg vises were popular. Then they began to fade from view as metal vises became cheap thanks to mass-manufacturing. Instead of having to build a leg vise from scratch, you could bolt an iron vise to your bench and be done inside of an hour.

When I built my first leg vise, I kept looking for its fatal functional flaw, but I didn't find one. Here are its advantages: It's simple and can be user-made with just a commercial screw and scraps. It doesn't have any parallel-guide bars. Therefore it can hold tapered objects quite well. It can clamp objects anywhere between the jaw and the bench's leg. This comes in handy quite a bit.

Downsides: Simple versions require a parallel guide. This is a stick of wood below the screw that is pierced with a lot of holes and passes freely through a mortise in the leg. When you place a steel pin through a hole, the vise's jaw pivots on the pin as it hits the leg of the bench. This is what gives the vise its fantastic holding power. The downside

TWO METHODS TO ADJUST A LEG VISE
A TAPERED SCRAP OF WOOD (LEFT) CAN PROVIDE THE OPPOSING FORCE NEEDED
TO CLAMP THE WORK. A PARALLEL GUIDE (RIGHT) IS THE MORE COMMON
OPTION.

is you must move the pin when you switch from clamping a drawer to clamping a 3/4"-thick panel.

But it's not as often as you might think. I thought I'd be moving the pin constantly when going from 1/2"-thick to 3/4"-thick work, but those thicknesses used the same hole in my parallel guide. Instead, you move it when you make larger jumps in thickness.

There are several ways to eliminate a parallel guide. The X-shaped mechanism mentioned above (commercially sold as a Benchcrafted Crisscross) does the job best. Alternately, you can use a closely fit round shaft that passes through a hole in the leg. When the jaw encounters the work, the shaft tilts and wedges in the hole in the leg (like a holdfast).

Another option: You can install a second screw at the floor and have a plate that spins on the screw. That movable plate acts like the movable pin in a parallel guide. This is handy because you can spin the plate forward and back with your toe.

Or you can skip the parallel guide altogether, which is how A.J. Roubo shows it in his 18th-century book. I worked this way for more than a year and used tapered scraps of wood and whatnot to tilt the jaw to hold the work. It's simple. It works. But it's occasionally frustrating when the right-size scrap is not immediately at hand.

My favorite setup? No question. A Crisscross.

Now that we're into leg vises, you might wonder if a steel or wooden screw is better. I don't have a preference. A big wooden screw moves incredibly fast – as fast as a typical double-lead steel screw. Wooden screws can get swollen and broken when grossly mistreated (they also can last centuries when treated with care). Steel screws can rust. And the hardware – secured with bolts or screws – can become loose (but also can last centuries if taken care of).

Steel screws typically see far too much lubrication (yes, that sentence was difficult to write), especially from oil or grease that eventually gets dirty. This gunk can then easily mar your work. To remedy this, remove the screw (and its nut). Degrease them both and lubricate the screw with a little graphite. It's then unlikely the screw will mark your work.

The leg vise was one of my biggest worries when "Workbenches: From Design & Theory to Construction & Use" was released in 2007. To be fair, I was worried about a lot of things, and I was braced for a toddler-style slap fight with the Internet. The entire book revolved around two obsolete workbench designs. Both were made with construction softwood. Oh, and both benches were powered by the little-used leg vise.

When the book came out, I didn't know anyone else in the world who had used a leg vise.

Instead of getting eviscerated, something worse happened. For months, I didn't hear anything. Not just crickets. Crickets with ball gags.

I actually visited local bookstores to see if my book was there. It wasn't. Had it really been distributed? Perhaps the bookstores didn't want it?

Then something changed. It started with people like a retired judge down in Alabama I met last year. He'd read the book when it first

CRISSCROSS REPLACES A PARALLEL GUIDE
BASED ON EXAMPLES FROM THE 19TH CENTURY, THE BENCHCRAFTED CRISSCROSS PROVIDES THE OPPOSING FORCE AUTOMATICALLY.

WORKHOLDING: EDGES & ENDS

came out and was intrigued. He bought the yellow pine and built the Roubo bench.

"It was the best damn thing in the world" he told me. "It worked perfectly."

He and fellow brave souls who read the book told their woodworking friends. They showed off their benches to visitors. And that's when the book started to sell. Soon people began sending me photos of their benches, as proud as if they were pictures of their firstborn.

Ideas and words are never enough. The ideas have to be dragged out and poked with a stick to see if there's any life in them. And that takes time.

I was also relieved that I hadn't just stuck a quick-release vise on the front of the two benches in the book. That was one of my original "make the people like me" plans.

WOODEN-JAWED FACE VISE

Some benches use a leg vise that has been rotated 90° to create a large face vise. This vise can have a wooden screw with a parallel guide that runs in a track directly below the benchtop and (typically) to the left of the screw in a right-handed bench. Or the vise can have metal parallel bars and a metal screw. This sort of vise carries all the sorts of caveats and variations as the leg vise. Its advantage is you don't need a big bench leg that is coplanar with the front edge of the benchtop. (So you can have a trestle base where the legs are tucked under the benchtop.)

One upside to this type of vise compared to a leg vise: No stooping. One downside: you don't get the nice clamping action between the leg and jaw that is sometimes helpful.

TWIN-SCREW VISE

One variation on the wooden-jawed face vise described above is to replace the parallel guide with a second screw. Most people call it a twin-screw vise, and it is a wonderful thing. If the screws have 24" of space between them, clamping a carcase side for dovetailing is easy. You also can use one screw to act as a parallel guide for the other to create some impressive clamping pressure. You can clamp tapered bits with ease.

What's the disadvantage? The twin-screw vise can be positioned too low for healthy dovetailing. You might end up bent over the vise to cut

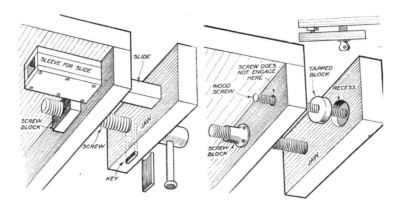

WOODEN-JAWED FACE VISE

THIS VISE FROM CHARLES HAYWARD WORKS SIMILARLY TO A LEG VISE. THE OPPOSING FORCE IS PROVIDED BY A SLIDE OR WOODEN SCREW.

your dovetails and experience fatigue or pain. I do love the twin-screw vise, but I prefer to make it a separate vise – what I call a Moxon vise – to elevate the work 6" or so off the benchtop for sawing or planing.

There are metal and wooden versions of the twin-screw vise. Some use a bicycle chain to link the two screws. Some have independent screws. I prefer the independent screws. Even though it might seem more fiddly to clamp and unclamp the work, they have less maintenance than twin-screws that are linked with a chain. I've taken several of these chain-driven vises apart for maintenance. Simpler is definitely better in this case.

METAL QUICK-RELEASE VISES

It's hard to argue with a quick-release vise. It's easy to install. It can slide easily right up to your work. It can clamp like the dickens. So, what's not to like?

The parallel bars and the small size of its jaw.

On either side of the screw are round metal bars that allow the vise to slide open and closed easily. These need to be kept clean and nearly tight to work well. But keeping rust at bay isn't the major problem with these vises. Instead, it's the fact that they impede clamping. On a large

WORKHOLDING: EDGES & ENDS

WOODEN TWIN-SCREW VISE

These are ideal for clamping wide panels for dovetailing.

VERITAS TWIN-SCREW VISE

This clever vise links the two screws with a bicycle-style chain. The added complexity adds some maintenance.

JORGENSEN QUICK-RELEASE VISE
Steel screws and grease tend to attract sawdust. The front and rear of the screw are quite dirty.

quick-release vise you might only get 3" of jaw outside the parallel bars. Sorry, but 3" is crap for dovetailing an 8" x 18" drawer side (never mind a 20"-wide x 40"-long carcase side).

Yes, you can trick these vises into doing much more with some bar clamps and other cleverness. You can also add a wooden jaw to increase their clamping capacity. I contend that the quick-release vise is more suited for metalworkers and machinists who need to hold small bits of work. The vises don't excel at holding big panels in most instances.

Also, a note about the life of these vises during the long-term: I've had my grandfather's quick-release vise for almost 30 years. It's a quality Jorgensen. Among all the vises I own, it requires the most maintenance and cleaning. Keeping the quick-release mechanism clean and functioning is important. And keeping the parallel bars clean of rust, lubricated and tight is important in a humid Midwestern environment.

My bottom line with these vises is that if you inherit them, they

WORKHOLDING: EDGES & ENDS

OLIVER PATTERNMAKER'S VISE
THESE HEAVY AND COMPLEX VISES ARE OVERKILL FOR MANY FURNITURE-MAKING OPERATIONS, BUT THE VISES REMAIN POPULAR WITH PEOPLE WHO WORK WITH UNUSUAL SHAPES.

are definitely worth using. Just know their limitations. If you have a choice, however, there are vises better suited for furniture making.

ABOUT THAT PATTERNMAKER'S VISE

If you work with odd shapes, tapered or round bits of wood, a patternmaker's vise might be a godsend. But if you are a normal woodworker who makes lots of boxes with only occasional curved and round shapes, the patternmaker's vise is a bit like owning a Ferrari for driving to Creamy Whip.

Its tapering jaws, tilting capacity and integral dogs hold lots of odd shapes indeed. But the vise is expensive, a pain to install and sometimes has to be removed to flatten the workbench top. It's a special tool for special applications. It's not my first, second or third choice for a furniture maker.

Oh, but look at that photo. I own one. A nice one that has been pro-

SLIDING DEADMAN
THIS SLIDING DEADMAN, SOMETIMES CALLED A BOARD JACK, HELPS SUPPORT
LONG BOARDS AND BIG WORKPIECES, SUCH AS DOORS.

fessionally restored. So I should just shut the hell up.

ACCESSORIES FOR WORKING ON EDGES & ENDS

Sometimes a face vise alone is not enough to get the job done when working on edges and ends. For long boards, the face vise might not have enough holding power to keep the work immobile as you plane it or mortise it.

To add support from below, consider adding a sliding deadman (or make it curvy and call it a deadwoman), a mobile board jack or some holdfasts in the far leg. If you have an English-style workbench with a wide front apron (aka a Nicholson), put pegs in the apron to support the work.

Sometimes working on the edges of boards happens on the benchtop – not in the face vise. You might end up planing edges against a planing stop. Or you can use a series of pegs in the benchtop to support a board on edge. This trick I picked up from the book "Woodworking in Estonia."

Finally, it's always a good idea to enhance the grip of the jaws of your face vise. I've tried a lot of materials. Here they are listed from least favorite to favorite:

• Cork shelf-paper liner. This is cheap and easy to apply – just peel and stick. But it gets chewed up quickly. Luckily, it's also easy to remove or replace.

• Cork and rubber gasket material. Farm supply stores carry sheets of rubberized gasket material that is ground up rubber and cork. (You can also buy this from Benchcrafted as "Crubber" and at auto-parts stores as "cork-rubber" in the gasket section.) This is way more durable than cork alone. There are lots of ways to stick it to the jaws of your vises. I prefer epoxy.

• Suede. My favorite liner for vise jaws is a coarse, nappy suede. It's also the most expensive option. I affix it to the vise jaws using epoxy or hide glue (if the surface is wood). Gluing leather using hide glue is like reassembling the cow (in my sick mind). Suede has the advantage of being a material made from natural and interlocked fibers (much like wood). So it's quite durable.

PLANING STOP MADE BY TOM LATANE, 2020
Since Roman times, the toothed planing stop has been an important part of workholding on the benchtop.

CHAPTER IX
WORKHOLDING: FACES OF BOARDS

When it comes to working on the faces of boards placed on a benchtop, the arguments about the workholding sound a lot like my wife and I jousting about car transmissions. Which should we buy: automatic or stick shift?

In the world of workbenches, the automatic transmission is a tail vise (or wagon vise) that's coupled with a system of dogs. With the twist of a screw, you can pinch the work between dogs to hold it for planing, chopping, carving or sanding.

The stick shift of workholding is a lone planing stop – basically a stick in a hole with some nails sticking out (in its most primitive iteration). It's simple as heck, and it takes some skill to use. Your first attempts will feel awkward (you might even fail). But once you master it, you won't require a tail vise.

There is no single correct approach. In fact, our workshop (which sometimes feels like a workbench laboratory) reflects the complex world of vises out there. We have nine different workbenches in the front room of our shop (plus a shavehorse and a portable workbench). Seven of the benches have a vise at one end that allows the user to pinch the work between dogs.

Though we have a lot of end vises in the shop, I almost never use them in my work. Why not? To be honest, they slow me down. Once I got the hang of working with a planing stop and a couple holdfasts, I never felt the urge to crank open a tail vise. That is the honest truth. And I'm not a historical reenactor or someone who can afford to waste time at the bench. My income comes from making furniture and writing about it. I work at my bench (or someone else's bench when I teach) every day.

But I don't simply dismiss all end vises. Some people adore them and wouldn't trade them for anything. (And they have their advantages when gripping pieces that don't sit flat on the bench or need to be worked at odd angles.)

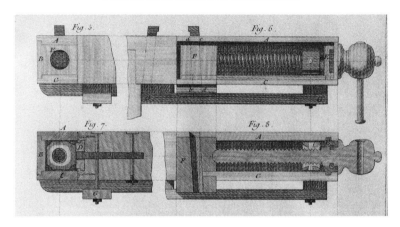

ROUBO'S TAIL VISE, PLATE 279, 18ᵗʰ CENTURY
The tail vise in Roubo is similar to many German forms of the time.

Instead, my point is that I don't want you to think that every workbench has to have an end vise as standard equipment. It doesn't. The first known end vise shows up in the written record in 1505 (it is a wagon vise drawn in a Germanic codex). And people were working wood just fine for many centuries before that.

So, let's get into some nitty gritty details about the different kinds of end vises, both the pros and the cons.

EUROPEAN TAIL VISE: THE MOVING BOX

This is the classic and most common style of tail vise. It's a dovetailed box that slides left and right on a screw. The box is pierced with dog holes. And the end of the box is a clamping surface – you can pinch work between the box and the benchtop.

It has some real advantages. The clamping area between the box and the benchtop allows you to add other vises (such as an Etaux), and it is an ideal place to hold rails for cutting tenons and for dovetailing small components (it actually functions as a pretty fair face vise). The vise allows you to disassemble frames and boxes by putting the bench's dogs inside a door assembly (for example) and opening the vise jaw to pull the parts apart.

WORKHOLDING: FACES OF BOARDS

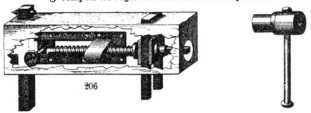

LA FORGE ROYALE TAIL VISE, 20ᵀᴴ CENTURY
After almost 200 years, little has changed in the mechanism for a tail vise.

TAIL VISE IN USE
The gap between the benchtop and the tail vise is an effective clamping area, especially for dovetailing small drawer parts and cutting tenons.

THE ANARCHIST'S WORKBENCH

When it comes to clamping boards flat on the benchtop, it works fine – when the vise is well-maintained. (Note that the only vise that doesn't require maintenance is one that is still in the box.) Many of the tail vises I have used through the years have been abused or neglected.

The abuse? The movable box is a "no mallet" zone. Striking work that is on top of the box will encourage it to sag. The neglect? The vise was either hastily installed or its mounting screws have come loose, allowing the box to sag.

The sagging box is annoying. When you clamp a board between dogs with a sagging box, the dog in the box will tend to lift your work off the bench. Then you have to knock the dog (or work) down to get it flat on the bench. But wait – the area is supposed to be a "no mallet" zone, so hitting things there tends to make the problem worse.

To be fair, there are tail vises that have been installed well and are made to avoid sagging. If you want to go with this form of vise, check out plans that have the hardware secured in a wooden groove on both components. Just screwing the hardware to a flat surface isn't good enough in my experience.

Aside from the maintenance, I'm also not generally a fan of clamping between dogs. It's slower. If you have pieces of wood that are all different lengths, then you have to move the dogs and screws to accommodate the different lengths. That's not a problem when using a planing stop.

Another caution about tail vises: If you clamp a board with a tad too much pressure, it will bow up in its center. You can't plane that board flat. So, you have to be a little sensitive. This is not a big deal once you know how little pressure is needed.

Other differences: Some people like to plane up mouldings with the work pinched between dogs. I prefer a sticking board – a bench appliance dedicated to mouldings that also provides sideways support that you don't get with a tail vise.

Other people like to traverse boards gripped with a tail vise – if you have metal dogs with serrated teeth it can hold work like the devil. I prefer to use a holdfast and a doe's foot (a stick of wood with a notch in it) or some other method.

And on and on the debate goes. So honestly, no one is going to win this argument. If you want a tail vise, buy the best and install it so it cannot sag. Then name the thing "Chrissy" after me and laugh every time you use it. That's cool by me.

WORKHOLDING: FACES OF BOARDS

IMPROVISED STICKING BOARD IN USE
A SIMPLE STICKING BOARD IS FASTER THAN PINCHING THE WORK BETWEEN DOGS IN MANY CASES.

WAGON VISE

THIS HOMEMADE WAGON VISE WAS CONSTRUCTED WITH A SCREW INTENDED FOR A VENEER PRESS.

THE WAGON VISE

A wagon vise is basically a tail vise that doesn't sag. Its downside is it doesn't have the same ability to clamp objects between the box and the benchtop (like the European tail vise above). There are several manufacturers that make wagon vises, and I like them all.

I've installed a lot of them, and the installation is the only thing I'm not wild about. You have to cut a (sometimes complex-shaped) cavity in the benchtop. Or create one as you laminate the boards together for the benchtop. You (usually) also have to add an end cap to the benchtop to hold the vise hardware. So, there's some up-front head-scratching and fiddling. But once the thing is installed, it's more low-maintenance than the European tail vise. Just keep the mechanism clean and lubricated.

It clamps boards without sagging. It doesn't create a "no mallet" zone. On the downside, it will (obviously) bow boards if you clamp them too tightly.

WORKHOLDING: FACES OF BOARDS

QUICK-RELEASE VISE USED AS END VISE
A QUICK-RELEASE VISE BOLTED TO THE END OF THE BENCHTOP CAN SERVE AS AN EFFECTIVE TAIL VISE.

During the last 15 years, I've made a variety of these vises from scratch and used the commercial versions. I think it gets an A for functionality. Installing them is about a C.

Despite all my grumbling above, the wagon vise is my favorite end vise.

QUICK-RELEASE VISES AT THE END OF THE BENCH

By installing a quick-release vise on the end of your benchtop – instead of on the front edge – you can transform it into an effective end vise. It seems like an ideal fix. The vise is easy to install. It doesn't sag (if bolted in place with through-bolts, nuts and washers). And it moves nimbly thanks to its quick-release function.

But it does have downsides. First, its standard dog is located in the middle of the vise's metal jaw, which could be 8" wide (or wider). That puts your line of bench dogs 4" away (or more) from the front edge of the benchtop. You will be happier if the dogs are closer to the front edge. About 2" is a good distance. This allows you to clamp pieces to

VERITAS WONDER DOG
THIS SIMPLE SURFACE VISE ALLOWS YOU TO PINCH WORK ALMOST ANYWHERE.
IT IS NOT IDEAL FOR WORKING WITH THIN PIECES.

the benchtop and easily use "fenced planes" (handplanes with fences, such as plows or moving fillisters). When the work is hanging off the front edge of the benchtop, the plane's fence won't encounter the benchtop.

To get the clamping near the front edge, I install a wooden chop that is attached to the movable jaw of the vise. I install a dog in that wooden chop near the front edge of the benchtop. That allows me to clamp work close to its front edge. The wooden jaw reduces the amount you can open the vise jaws. But (on the plus side) you now have a wooden jaw in the vise, and that won't mar any work that you clamp there.

Putting a quick-release vise on the end of the benchtop is my second-favorite end vise. It gets a B for functionality and a B for ease of installation.

WORKHOLDING: FACES OF BOARDS

DIFFERENT TYPES OF BENCH DOGS
WOODEN, METAL, ROUND AND SQUARE. EACH TYPE HAS ITS ADVANTAGES AND DISADVANTAGES.

SURFACE VISES

Another end vise is a surface vise. This retrofits to any workbench (or even just a 2x12). First drill a series of holes for dogs. Put a dog in one hole. Put the surface vise in another hole. The surface vise has a movable pressure plate that allows you to clamp your work like any tail vise.

The upside: It's easy to install. The downside: It's unsuited for planing thin pieces of stock. The jaw of the surface vise sticks up above the benchtop and cannot be moved down like a dog. So if the jaw is 5/8" thick, then you can't (easily) plane anything 5/8" thick or thinner. Yes, there are clever workarounds. Yes, they are fiddly.

If you only plane up thick stock (3/4" thick or thicker), then a vise such as this is fine. Otherwise, it's quite limiting.

SQUARE VS. ROUND VS. WOOD VS. METAL

If you do decide to install an end vise, you have to choose between

THE ANARCHIST'S WORKBENCH

TOOTHED PLANING STOP
A METAL PLANING STOP CAN BE ADDED TO A WORKBENCH YEARS LATER. YOU JUST NEED TO MORTISE A HOLE IN THE BENCHTOP.

round dogs vs. square dogs. And whether they should be metal or wood.

Round dogs are easy to install (just drill a hole), but they rotate easily, which can be wildly convenient or inconvenient, depending on the task at hand. Square dogs require a square and stepped mortise in the benchtop, which is pretty easy to install while building the bench but is pretty much a pain in the butt to install after the bench is complete.

So, make up your mind before you start building the bench.

Many metal dogs hold better because they have serrated clamping faces. But these faces also tend to mar the work. (Marring the work is not always a big deal. In fact, some people consider it a mark of hand craftsmanship.) On the downside, metal dogs will wreck your handplane if the two should collide.

WORKHOLDING: FACES OF BOARDS

Wooden dogs don't hold as well. But the plane wins when a wooden dog and handplane try to occupy the same airspace.

There is no clear choice when it comes to the shape of your dogs and material they are made from. Pick a style and learn to work with it. All four types work and exist in the historical record. So, someone out there has made the same mistake/brilliant decision as you. Sleep easy.

PLANING STOPS

I think every bench should have a planing stop. There is no downside to having one. They are easy to install. They don't cost a lot of money (if any). They can change your woodworking.

Historically, a planing stop is a stick of wood that's 3" x 3" x 12". It is friction-fit into a mortise in the benchtop about 3" from the front edge of the bench near where the face vise is located. Just make sure the mortise doesn't interfere with the structure below the benchtop or force you to reach awkwardly over the face vise while planing.

You adjust the planing stop up and down with mallet strikes. The stop has metal teeth, or it can have a V-shaped block of wood I call a "palm." These teeth can come from a manufactured planing stop that is installed in the end of the wood. Or the teeth can be the points of nails driven through the wooden stop.

Either way, metal teeth will mar the work, which can be a plus or a minus depending on your perspective on historical tool marks.

The advantage to the metal teeth is that it prevents boards from rocking or shifting on the bench. If you have a board with twist, knock one end into the teeth (hard!) and it won't move as you plane out the twist. The teeth also assist you when you are planing boards on edge on the benchtop. Sometimes the planing stop will be 6" above the workbench and the metal tooth will prevent the board from tipping over as you work with it.

When planing pieces that are thin or long, knock them into the teeth to keep them from skittering around. If you have a thin board that is bowed, place the concave face up and drive one end into the stop's teeth. Then let gravity and the weight of the tool hold things as you plane the board. (Note: this cleans up the board but won't flatten it.)

When you use it, you first decide if you are going to mallet the work into the teeth from behind the board to get some extra grip. If the

DRIVING A BOARD INTO THE TEETH
Your work will teeter less on the benchtop if you drive the end grain into the teeth of the planing stop.

PLANING STOP MADE WITH NAILS
A typical and inexpensive planing stop uses nails driven through the movable block.

WORKHOLDING: FACES OF BOARDS

board is flat and well behaved, press it against the teeth of the planing stop and go to work. The teeth will mark the work a little. If the board is wonky, use a mallet to drive the board into the teeth. Then your work will stay fairly fixed.

The planing stop also serves as the foundation for other accessories. Place a 6"-wide and thin piece of stock across the benchtop and against the stop. Secure the far end with a holdfast. Now you have a wide planing stop for working on panels.

The stop also serves as the stop for a sticking board for making mouldings. And it's also a stop when planing up anything in a cradle. I have cradles for making octagonal and hexagonal legs. The planing stop restrains the cradle and the work.

For traversing, make an accessory called a "doe's foot." The doe's foot is a piece of stock, typically 1/2" thick or a little thinner. It's maybe 6" wide and 24" long. It has a 90° birdsmouth cut into one end. All of these dimensions are adjustable based on your work.

Here's how to use it. Place your work firm against the planing stop. Put the notch of the doe's foot around the far corner of the other end of the board. Secure the doe's foot with a holdfast (or a clamp). That's it. The doe's foot prevents the work from rotating when you plane across the grain, diagonally or with the grain.

What are the downsides to the planing stop? Many woodworkers have expressed fear they will cut their hand on the teeth. I'm sure it has happened, but I haven't had it happen to a student or to me. If you are freaked out about having a sharp piece of metal on your benchtop, perhaps you should give your chisels away to charity. Same thing.

If you have concerns, here are a couple remedies: Cut a shallow recess in the benchtop to keep the teeth below the benchtop when the stop isn't in use. Second remedy: Dull the teeth a bit with a file until you get used to its presence. The stop won't be as effective, but it will still work.

Installing a planing stop involves cutting a deep mortise through the benchtop (or building it into the laminations when you glue up the benchtop). Then you fit the stop to the mortise. Use the driest stock possible for the stop. During the first year, the benchtop might shrink or swell. You might have to plane the long edges of the stop to get it to move easily again. You might have to shim the interior of the mortise a tad if the stop moves too easily. Or you might have to make a

DOE'S FOOT IN USE

THE DOE'S FOOT PREVENTS THE BOARD FROM ROTATING WHEN YOU PLANE ACROSS THE GRAIN OR PARALLEL TO THE GRAIN.

WORKHOLDING: FACES OF BOARDS

VERSATILE PLANING STOP
THIS SIMPLE APPLIANCE ALLOWS YOU TO PLANE WIDE AND THICK STOCK WITH EASE.

new wooden stop. None of these problems are real problems. Once the bench settles down, the stop will as well.

One last word on planing stops. If you aren't sure if you want one, make a planing stop that can clamp in your face vise. It's simply a thick chunk of wood screwed to a thinner board in an L shape. Clamp the thick bit in the vise; the thinner board lies across the benchtop. And now you have a planing stop, and it's adjustable up and down, too.

OTHER STOPS

When you are backed into a corner, sometimes you need to screw (or nail) a stop to your benchtop or the front edge of the bench. This isn't my first choice, but I seem to do it a couple times a year for expediency.

Some woodworkers make their benches with a split top. I've worked on many of these benches (I've not built one). The integrated tool-holder/wide planing stop is nice for traversing – as long as you aren't trying to plane up a wide case side. The stop is in the middle of

THE ANARCHIST'S WORKBENCH

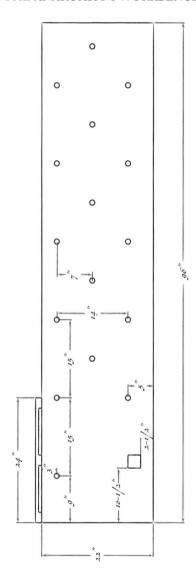

HOLDFAST HOLE PATTERN
THIS DIAGRAM SHOWS THE PATTERN OF HOLDFAST HOLES I PREFER.

WORKHOLDING: FACES OF BOARDS

the bench, and case sides can be 18" to 20" wide.

My only other criticisms of split-top benchtops are:

They add a little complexity during construction or require some additional parts, depending on the style of bench you are building.

The two tops can move or warp differently. I worked on one that had this problem and I simply had to do all my work on the front slab.

Occasionally your small tools, screws and bits of hardware will roll into that split. It's the Split-top Law.

The last stop system I'll mention is one that shows up in early benches, especially in Germany. They feature an array of pegs on the benchtop that you can knock up and down. Some can act as planing stops. Some can act as side stops. Some can be used for traversing the work. We have this system on a bench in our shop and it works well.

HOLDFASTS

I thought about devoting an entire chapter to holdfasts – they are that important to my work. Then I realized that holdfasts work so simply that it would be the shortest chapter in the book.

Holdfasts themselves are a simple friction clamp. Strike the shaft from above and it cinches down. Strike the shaft from behind and it releases. You can use holdfasts directly on the work (with a pad to protect the work) or they can restrain stops or accessories (such as a doe's foot or a batten).

The biggest question with holdfasts is where to put the holes. I don't think the best answer is: Anywhere you like. I have spent a lot of time and energy figuring out an array of holes that work – without making your bench a holy mess.

The diagram shows where I prefer my holdfast holes. There is one hole near the single-point planing stop for restraining a wide planing stop. The rest of the holes are in three rows that allow you to restrain a doe's foot or accessories such as a Moxon vise. The holes in the diagram are spaced for a holdfast with a typical reach of 7".

The array shown gives you almost complete coverage of the benchtop without a lot of unnecessary boring. So, begin with this array before you start putting holes willy-nilly through the benchtop.

HOLDFASTS & DOE'S FEET AT WORK
YOU WILL BE SURPRISED BY WHAT YOU CAN HOLD WITH A PAIR OF HOLDFASTS AND DOE'S FEET, SUCH AS THIS CREST RAIL.

WORKHOLDING: FACES OF BOARDS
KEEP IT SIMPLE

Because I used to have a public email address and phone number, and because I wrote a book titled "Workbenches," I heard a lot of questions from would-be workbench builders. Also, workbench theorists. And workbench crackpots.

For every simple workholding method, there are 10 more that involve a compressor, a Venturi chamber, a series of rubber bladders and conveyor belts.

Plus, I fought this fight during every class I taught.

I preach simple benches. Or to be more precise: You should start simple and go from there.

But there were always a few students who didn't want a simple bench. They wanted a ridiculous bench with two face vises, a tail vise and a wagon vise. Oh, and all the vises were different brands.

They wanted four rows of dog holes. Why?

"I saw it once. It looks useful."

"It's not," I say.

"OK, I think it will help the benchtop respond to changes in relative humidity."

"It won't," I say.

"OK, I just want it."

At first, these debates discouraged me. Then a switch flipped in my head, and I simply wallowed in wondering who would have the most ridiculous request during a class.

"You want to have both round and square dog holes leapfrogging each other? OK, you win."

During one of these many workbench classes, I remember tinkering with a router jig for the bench bolts we were using when my phone rang. About 30 seconds later, another switch flipped in my head, and I decided to quit corporate America.

'CHRISTUS HELPT JOZEF BIJ TIMMERMANSWERK,' 1649
ANOTHER WIERIX-STYLE BENCH FROM THE LOW COUNTRIES.

CHAPTER X
AFRAID OF FIRE

One of my biggest personality flaws can be explained with this simple story. I asked a blacksmith to make me a metal planing stop. He insisted that the best planing stops were made from railroad spikes and that he would charge me just $20 for the thing.

The box arrived, and I opened it. I took one look at the toothy and crusty metal stop and said: Nope. I refused to install it on the bench, and so my first adjustable planing stop was wooden. It worked OK. But I had absolutely no idea what I was missing until I installed a metal one two years and five months later.

I wonder sometimes: What is my malfunction? I could have installed the metal stop in an hour. If it didn't work, I could have made a replacement wooden one in a second hour.

This kind of crap – holding desperately onto something that works OK instead of taking a small step that could improve everything – is exactly what kept me immobilized in corporate America way past my expiration date.

From the day I entered the workforce as an adult in June 1990 until I said "I quit" to my boss at *Popular Woodworking* in 2011, I was intent on holding onto every job I had. Getting fired or laid off crossed my mind almost every day. And (even worse) that fear seemed to make all the important decisions in my career. A few highlights:

For five years I wrote freelance copy for the now-defunct Woodworker's Book Club and poured that money into my workshop at home. My rationale: I wanted to be ready to work as an independent furniture maker on the day that I got canned.

It wasn't the stupidest fear. Being a journalist these days is almost as irrelevant as being a wheelwright or the guy who makes coats from the foreskins of sperm whales (that's a real thing, by the way; you know I wouldn't lie to you re: whale dongs). But it did make me do stupid things.

My office at home was next to my daughters' bedrooms, and while

THE ANARCHIST'S WORKBENCH

RAILROAD SPIKE PLANING STOP
IT TOOK ME YEARS OF WAFFLING TO INSTALL THIS STOP IN MY WORKBENCH.

banging out meaningless monthly drivel for the Woodworkers' Book Club, Maddy would beg me to play "Baldur's Gate" with her on the computer. More often than not, I put her off in order to get the freelance work done on time. And so Maddy would wait for me in my office and she illustrated a little book (that I still own) titled "The Monsters of Baldur's Gate" containing advice for us.

Yeah, even then I felt like a crap parent. But I rationalized that all the freelance work would save us from future disaster. We wouldn't have to go back to the days when our checking account dipped below $100 every two weeks, right before payday.

Every month, I got a check from the Book Club. I put half away for taxes. The rest I spent on the tools I thought I needed for a one-bad-father furniture shop. For starters: a chop saw, drill press, spray finishing equipment, mortiser, compressor with many nail guns and a stupid jig for drilling shelf-pin holes. These weren't tools I really wanted to own. But they were tools I knew other furniture makers owned.

AFRAID OF FIRE

EARLY 2011 TOOL CHEST CLASS IN GERMANY
TEACHING CLASSES ALL OVER THE WORLD WAS ONE OF THE WAYS I PREPARED MYSELF FOR THE DAY I WOULD BE FIRED FROM MY CORPORATE JOB.

I'm not a prepper, but I think this is what it must feel like to put away 1,000 gallons of potable water and 300 cans of beans for the apocalypse. As my shop at home came together, I began to feel less anxious about being fired. I was ready.

One day one of my woodworking friends shut down his shop and went to work for his wife. Despite his talents (he's a better woodworker than I'll ever be), the work had dried up. The phone had stopped ringing. He had all of the tools (even a Timesaver wide-belt sander that was bigger than my truck). Plus, he had the skills and 20 years of experience. But nobody wanted to hire him.

This freaked me out. Owning the tools was not enough.

I started trolling around for commission furniture work, even if it didn't pay much. I decided I had to build a customer base. (Tools plus customers equals job security, right?) I began making Morris chairs and selling them on eBay. I started building pieces for my wife's boss, hoping he would spread my name among his wealthy friends. I even dabbled in trimming out a kitchen or two owned by friends in Cincinnati's Northside neighborhood.

So I was building furniture at night. On other evenings I was still writing copy for the Woodworker's Book Club. I hadn't picked up my guitar in years. And "Baldur's Gate" remained unsolved.

One week at work I received two phone calls that seemed like a gift. Marc Adams called to ask if I would teach at his school in Indiana. Then Kelly Mehler called to ask if I would teach at his school in Kentucky.

I said yes to both. Becoming a woodworking teacher was another layer of economic protection. I thought: Even if this bad thing happened and those other bad things happened, I also had teaching. I would be impossible to snuff out.

This is the point in the story where it should all come crashing down. But it doesn't.

One of the many reasons I started Lost Art Press was to have something else to fall back on – yes, another stopgap – for when I was finally fired at *Popular Woodworking*. That fear might seem irrational. My only defense is that magazine editors are flushed with more regularity than most people's bowels. Every year at *Popular Woodworking* I attended four or five going-away parties at bars for colleagues who had been canned.

The horror always seemed to be just around the corner. Even if you had 10 or 12 glowing yearly evaluations behind you *[Editor's note: Or 19]*, there was a decent chance that you'd soon be at the Buffalo Wild Wings on Lane Avenue, drunk and with your car's trunk full of your kids' drawings. Which used to decorate your cubicle.

So I worked. April became a bad month and a bitter family joke. My youngest daughter's birthday is at the end of April, and I missed it about five years in a row because I was teaching out of town.

OK, I know for certain that the narrative arc should now take us to the breaking point. It wasn't, however, a made-for-TV moment.

I was teaching a workbench class at Kelly Mehler's school in May of 2011 when my mom phoned me in the middle of class. I knew it was bad news. Her brother (my uncle), Thomas West, had just died. He was 71.

I wasn't close to my Uncle Tom. Instead I had always been in awe of him and was too timid to talk to him at the rare family gatherings.

He was the genius in the family and had a newsworthy career at Data General. Tracy Kidder wrote a Pulitzer-prize-winning book about him, "The Soul of a New Machine."

After my mother told me the news, I sat down. A switch had gone off in my head that I still cannot explain to this day.

I finished up the class and got into my truck to go home. I stopped at the Shell station down the road from Kelly's school to fill up my tank for the drive. I remember my hands shaking as I pulled the fuel nozzle from the truck.

I got in the car and called Lucy.

"I want to quit my job," I told her.

"OK," she said. "Come home, and we'll figure it out."

That was on a Friday evening. On Monday I turned in my resignation letter at the magazine. I think I was as shocked about the moment as my boss was.

All those years of preparing for the day – buying tools, building up a commission book, teaching, starting a company – none of that was helpful or comforting in that moment.

On my last day at the magazine, I loaded up the last of my tools. I plugged my phone into the stereo. It picked up where I'd left off in the morning with Superchunk's "Learning to Surf."

I should have quit years before I did. I know that now. The freelancing, teaching, commission work and publishing were all excuses. I thought: If I built this business, then I'd be ready. If I built that business, then I'd really be ready.

I had been ready for years but had been too chickenshit to write the resignation letter. I know this might seem like a "chicken and the egg" paradox, but I was an overcooked baby. I hid in the womb. And boy is my therapist gonna have a field day with this paragraph.

I drove home to my family and thought: Now I'm going to be a better father and husband. And I was. I picked up my kids from school every day. I was home for birthdays and graduations and the landmarks. I made dinner every night. (I still haven't finished "Baldur's Gate," however.)

This, I thought, is the reward for escaping the corporate world: More time with my family and the freedom to run my own life. But I was wrong. The real reward would come seven years later when my father lay dying.

THE ANARCHIST'S WORKBENCH

∧ ∧ ∧

At some point in my life, the following piece of trivia got lodged in my brain: There's sufficient evidence that the word "deadline" meant something fairly sinister in Confederate prisons during the U.S. Civil War. The "dead line" was literally a line marked in the ground to restrain prisoners. Cross the "dead line" and you would be shot.

This thought crossed my mind several times as I edited magazine stories and approved page layouts at the foot of my father's hospital bed after his first cancer surgery.

I was in downtown Chicago in the middle of winter trying, with the help of my sisters, to get my dad through the procedure in a city that was a world away from our Arkansas home.

I was also responsible for editing two woodworking magazines, one of which was just about to go on press.

My boss had, with great grace, allowed me to leave town to attend my dad's surgery. No questions and no complaints. The only catch was that I had to keep the magazine running. We couldn't miss printing deadlines. That's when things got royally screwed up and it began costing the company money.

There also is an unspoken rule at most media companies. If you miss hard deadlines, you will – sooner rather than later – be fired. No matter how good the content is that you produce, editors who blow deadlines are marked as difficult. And difficult editors are the first ones to go as soon as the magazine's budget or reputation hits the tiniest pebble.

Among the consultations with nurses and doctors I wrote an article about cutting tenons by hand. I approved about 100 pages of layouts. I edited an entire magazine issue with my laptop perched on my knees. I made dinner for my sisters. And I drove my dad back to Arkansas with his colostomy bag on the floorboards of my pickup truck.

When we pulled into town in Fort Smith, Ark., it was late, and my dad was craving fried chicken livers. I looked at him over the rim of my glasses.

"Really?" I asked.

The guy who ate sprouts and whole wheat bread for lunch every day wanted some fried organ meat?

AFRAID OF FIRE

PAUL SCHWARZ, HILL TOP LANE, ARK., 1970s
WE USED A SYSTEM OF ROPES TO RAISE THE FRAMED-UP WALLS, WHICH WERE BUILT FLAT ON THE FOUNDATION.

IN A CHAIR CLASS AT MIKE DUNBAR'S
My father took easily to any skill that required hand-eye coordination, including chairmaking and playing piano.

"I think I need the iron," he said.

I pulled into a Church's Chicken that had just closed for the night. In my hometown, white people don't go to Church's; we're supposed to go to KFC. So, I know it freaked out the employees when a long-haired bearded white dude banged on the door asking for chicken livers. The manager came to the door a little wary. I explained my problem.

He started up the deep fryer and made my dad a double order. Which dad gobbled up before we made it the two miles to his house.

I got my father into his bed, where he fell asleep immediately after an entire day in the car. I wasn't tired, and so I wandered around his house.

This wasn't the house I'd grown up in, but it was filled with the things my dad had made. There were the Japanese garden benches on his deck – a design of his so perfect that I ripped it off for a magazine article years later. There was the weird glass-topped coffee table that was made from about 120 pieces of redwood that had all been bolted together using all-thread – no glue.

I sat down in the living room and tried to decompress after the journey. And I noticed something new and curvy on the other side of the room. I walked over to investigate. It was a heating register made from wood, but it was handmade, pierced and carved with lovely curves. Who does that?

I knew the answer.

When I was a kid, my dad had built (and finished) furniture while confined to bedrest after some spinal surgery. He taught himself how to veneer furniture, build decorative brick walls and design houses (two of his original designs still stand today) before he was 40. He took piano lessons in his 50s. Vocal lessons in his 60s. Cello lessons in his 70s. If he wanted to do something, he just did it.

And here I was terrified of missing a printing deadline.

My dad and I were usually close. You would think that we'd be closer because we both loved making things. But we seemed to see handwork through different lenses. While he loved making things – furniture, music, pottery – it was the reward or the release after his difficult and meaningful work. My dad was a family physician.

For me, making things was the difficult and meaningful work. He wanted me to be a lawyer.

THE ANARCHIST'S WORKBENCH

After I quit my job at *Popular Woodworking* I didn't see my dad as much. He was building a new life in Charleston, S.C., and I was trying to forge a life as an independent furniture maker, writer, publisher and teacher. And trying to be a decent parent (if not a decent son).

In 2016, dad's cancer came roaring back. And that was when I knew I had made the right decision to leave the corporate world. After talking to my dad on the phone one evening, I said, "I'll be there tomorrow." I packed my bags and threw them in my truck. I didn't ask anyone for permission.

I just went. I didn't have any deadlines. Well, not for work.

When I arrived in Charleston the next afternoon my dad was impossibly skinny. He had converted to a vegan diet a few years before and was an insufferable evangelist about it, to boot.

"You hungry?" he asked. "I know a place."

During my previous visit the "place" was a Vietnamese gas station that served zero meat, eggs or dairy. In fact, I think they waited for the vegetables to drop off the vine before harvesting them.

We drove north on the peninsula to a neighborhood that had been crime ridden for decades. He pulled into a parking lot that was awash in the smell of brisket and smoked pork.

"Really?" I asked.

"It's going to change your life," he said.

We sat down in one of the booths and waited for lunch to arrive. And I waited for him to tell me exactly how bad things were with his cancer (they were bad). I had left my laptop and my phone in my truck or back at his house, where they would sit for a few days.

And then I did something I hadn't done since I was 5 or 6. I reached out across the table and grabbed his hand. He raised his eyebrows, smiled and nodded.

For the next eight months I drove to Charleston to visit him almost every month, taking turns with my sisters in taking care of him to the end.

Every time I packed my truck up for the trip, I had this same thought: I couldn't do this if I still had a corporate job. So, during my visits, instead of writing magazine stories while my father's health spiraled slowly downward, we watched "Jeopardy" and "Wheel of Fortune" every night together. I made him dinner (he gave up on veganism at his doctor's request; plus, he really wanted some brisket). And when he was feeling only half-horrible, we went to his favorite restaurants.

When he died, I was sitting on his bed with him and my sisters, singing his favorite Crosby, Stills & Nash songs. It's a morning that I will always be grateful for.

I'm not saying that quitting your job will make you a better person. But it did for me.

Today I still work damn hard. You have to when you work for yourself. In fact I work just as hard as I did when I had to meet my corporation's personal performance and financial goals, fearful of not being rated as "exceeds expectations." (My reward for exceeding expectations? A 3 percent merit raise. Yup, I worked every weekend so they could reward me with $2,400.)

But now I can turn my work off like a water faucet. When I want to take my daughter to the art museum, I just do it. When I feel the urge to hike the Red River Gorge with my family, I make the reservations that instant instead of checking to see how many days of PTO I have banked.

And when I want to build a workbench, I don't have to ask Steve for permission. I don't have to submit the plans for the bench to a bunch of people who really don't give a crap about traditional woodworking.

I just do it. And it's on the following page.

IMPROVED LEG VISE

One of the biggest changes to this bench is the leg vise. The jaw is twice as thick as before, and the screw is positioned lower. The Benchcrafted hardware is also a significant upgrade.

CHAPTER XI
INTRODUCTION TO
THE ANARCHIST'S WORKBENCH

After 20 years of thought, trial and experimentation, this workbench is where I have ended up.

I put the final coat of finish on it today, and I pushed it up against the first real workbench I built in 2000. Both are made using the same species of wood. Both have four legs, a shelf and an array of holes in the benchtop and legs. Neither has a tail vise.

To me the differences between the two benches are immense. In a glance I can see how every component has evolved during the intervening 20 years. The legs and top are thicker. The benchtop is narrower but longer. The joinery is completely different. My old bench is held together with nuts and bolts. You could take it apart with a ratchet set and a screwdriver. The new one is designed to come apart only with the help of a major house fire.

Before I designed the 2000 bench, I first amassed every workbench plan I could find at the library and in old magazines. I tried to design a bench that looked like it was the plausible offspring of all those other plans. I wanted people to say: Yup, he made a bench.

When I designed the bench for this book, I didn't look at anything except the paper on my clipboard as I drew its components. This bench, for better or for worse, is based on what I know will work.

That's not to say this bench is the ultimate this or the must-have that. It's not the end-all. Or even the "bed-busting sex" of workbenches. It's too simple to attract a lot of adjectives. What I can say is it's a design I've refined during many years. And millions of woodworkers refined it before me. I cannot think of any way to improve it.

THE BONES

This workbench has a 5"-thick top that is 22" wide and about 8' long. The legs are 5" x 5" – tree trunks compared to furniture components.

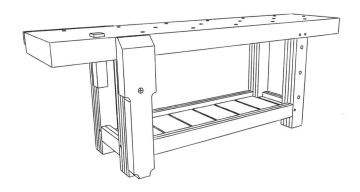

SIMPLE, BUT NOT TOO SIMPLE
THE BENCHTOP AND UNDERCARRIAGE ARE MADE ENTIRELY FROM 2X MATERIAL THAT HAS BEEN LAMINATED TOGETHER.

The stretchers are 2-1/2" thick and 4" wide.

The stretchers are 4" above the floor, which allows you to hook your foot under the front stretcher to pull yourself forward or brace yourself during some planing and sawing operations. The four stretchers enclose and support a shelf, which is essential for storing furniture parts, appliances and the like.

The benchtop is centered over its base with the front edge of the benchtop in the same plane as the front face of the legs and the front face of the long stretchers. This arrangement grants you great flexibility because you can clamp almost anything to the front of the bench – clamp your work to the benchtop, the legs, the stretchers. They are all in the same plane and welcome your clamps.

The top overhangs the base by 16" at both ends. This allows you a lot of room for clamping or adding a vise. Many bench designs have aprons or other structures that prevent a retrofit of an end vise or face vise without invasive surgery. This bench will accept many vises – no matter which woodworking tradition you hail from. So, you don't have to decide what vises you want immediately. You can change your mind later on. This design is "open format" (for lack of a better word) and can be adapted to your needs.

INTRODUCTION TO THE ANARCHIST'S WORKBENCH

A WORKBENCH IN THE ROUGH
ALL OF THE BOARDS FOR THIS BENCH WERE COLLECTED DURING A FEW
MONTH'S TIME AND WERE ALLOWED TIME TO DRY OUT.

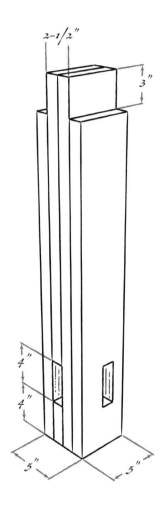

DETAILS OF LEG CONSTRUCTION
THE TENON AND ONE OF THE MORTISES IN THE LEG ARE CREATED WHILE GLUING UP THE LAMINATIONS.

INTRODUCTION TO THE ANARCHIST'S WORKBENCH

THE MAGIC 2X MATERIAL

All of the bench's thick components are created by laminating pieces of common 2x framing lumber together.

Here are the important details on framing lumber. When you go to the home center, you'll find 1x, 2x and 4x lumber (and maybe some 6x). Those numbers are supposed to indicate that the lumber mill started with bits of wood that were 1", 2", 4" and 6" thick then planed them down to the finished sizes, which are 3/4", 1-1/2", 3-1/2" and 5-1/2" thick.

We are concerned/obsessed with the 2x stuff. This is usually sold at 1-1/2" thick. But it's also warped and needs some drying time before you can use it in a workbench. With primo material, I can usually squeeze 1-3/8" thickness out of 2x material. But that is optimistic. When I am being realistic, I design pieces using 2x lumber and assume I can get the stuff flat, clean and 1-1/4" thick in the end.

And that 1-1/4" thickness is what all the components in this bench are based upon.

Even if you are a beginning woodworker, you will have no problem getting 2x material to 1-1/4" thickness unless your stock is firewood-in-waiting. You can do this by hand or with simple machines – a basic electric jointer and thickness planer are godsends when dealing with 2x material. And if you can get everything to 1-1/4" thick, then the rest of this workbench makes mathematical sense.

(Side note: The bench is designed to be made with an inexpensive 6" jointer and 12" thickness planer. You can't get more basic than that.)

The 5"-thick legs are made from four layers of 1-1/4"-thick material. To make the 2-1/2"-thick tenon on the top of the legs, we make the two center layers longer, creating the tenon.

The stretchers are 2-1/2" thick and made from two 1-1/4"-thick layers. And we'll make the 3"-long tenons on the ends by making one lamination 6" shorter than the other and centering it on the other pieces.

The mortises can be made by subtracting layers in some instances. You can easily make the mortise for the planing stop in the benchtop this way. You also can make half the mortises in the legs for the stretchers. (Wait, half? You'll figure it out.) Or you can bore or chop out all the mortises if you like. I don't think either method is superior to the other. I'm going to show both techniques.

WHY I LIKE 2X12S

When I build workbenches from framing lumber, I almost always buy 2x12s (which are 1-1/2" x 11-1/4"). A 2x12 can be ripped down its middle to give me two sticks that are ideal for the benchtop or the legs – about 5-1/2" wide each so I can plane them down to 5".

I could buy 2x10s for the stretchers, but I usually stick to the 2x12s for these as well. Why? I save the knottier 2x12s for the stretchers because I need only 4"-wide material – not 5". That gives me some flexibility when I have less-than-perfect material.

If you drive a massive truck and have a friend, be sure to poke through the 16'-long 2x12s as they tend to be clearer than the 8'-, 10'- or 12'-long sticks. To be honest, I have a small truck and don't always visit the lumberyard with friends, so I poke through the racks of 8'- and 10'-long 2x12s because I can handle them alone.

Here's another tip: Some yards stock No. 2 yellow pine; others stock No. 1. There is a price difference. But in my neck of the woods (Kentucky) it's only a $2 upcharge for a No. 1 grade 2x12. After you see the difference, you will believe me when I say that No. 2 is indeed No. 2. Don't be fooled by No. 2 Prime. It's still No. 2 wearing a tuxedo.

No. 1 has remarkably fewer knots and straighter grain. If you are measuring wood by the pound, No. 1 costs 2 cents more per pound than No. 2. Put another way, if you make a 300-pound workbench, using No. 1 for the whole thing will add $6 to the bill.

You might be wondering how much this workbench weighs. Before assembling the bench, I weighed the individual components on a heavy-duty scale we use for shipping crates of furniture. Without the vises and seat – just the pine – the bench weighs 307 lbs. The vise hardware and maple jaw add 29 lbs. The swing-away seat adds 17 lbs. Total: 353 lbs.

Your bench will weigh more or less, depending on the boards you pick at the lumberyard. Yellow pine varies quite a bit depending on how much of the heavy summerwood is in the board. Summerwood is the dense, dark orange annular rings. The whitish wood, the springwood, is spongier.

To illustrate the difference that's possible, I weighed the six shelf

INTRODUCTION TO THE ANARCHIST'S WORKBENCH

boards individually for the bench, which varied quite a bit in their proportion of summerwood (aka latewood) to springwood (aka earlywood). The lightest shelf board (1-1/4" x 9" x 17") weighed 3.5 lbs. The heaviest one weighed 4.8 lbs., or 37 percent more. So you can vary the final weight of your bench quite a bit simply by picking boards that are more orange at the lumberyard.

BECOME A 2X COLLECTOR

I'm not a wood hoarder, except when it comes to 2x12s. Every time I need a filter for my shop vacuum, blue tape or glue, I swing through the framing lumber section of the lumberyard and dig. I look for perfect boards that are straight and knot-free. If I can find a perfect board within five minutes of digging, I throw it on my cart. I typically find one board. Sometimes I get three or four, especially if the yard stocks No. 1.

When home, I pile the perfect specimens on top of the other 2x12s in the basement. When I have a bench-sized pile, I make a bench or a couple sawbenches. This might take months; it might take a year. Either way, it gives the wood plenty of time to dry and assume its final shape before I plane and saw it up. Patience pays.

WORKHOLDING

The workholding on this bench is simple and robust. The face vise is a leg vise with a metal screw and a X-shaped mechanism. (The hardware is made by Benchcrafted in Iowa. I used its Classic vise hardware and its Crisscross mechanism.) The movable wooden jaw is 3-1/4"-thick maple. I like the way maple looks for a vise chop. If you like you can use yellow pine and glue up three layers to create the chop.

I chose a metal screw for the vise because it is easy to install and moves quickly. I also love wooden vise screws. They require more woodworking to get the vise nut mortised into the leg, and you need to install a garter in the chop. That's not a big deal – I've done it many times. But in this instance the metal screw won by a hair.

The vise screw is positioned lower on the vise chop than most modern benches, which are usually 8" from the benchtop. This is intentional. Old workbenches had screws that were much lower – sometimes 12" to 15" below the benchtop. This increased the capacity of the vise – you could get wider boards in the jaws with ease. But you have to

THE ANARCHIST'S WORKBENCH

PLANING STOP BY TOM LATANE
I THINK MY FAVORITE DETAIL OF THIS UTILITARIAN WORKBENCH DESIGN IS THE FANCY PLANING STOP.

stoop more to work the vise.

After working with a bench for years with a 13" capacity above the screw, I didn't want to give that all up. That's why the vise screw on this bench is so low (it has 11" of clamping capacity above its screw). It might look weird. But that's because you have seen a lot of modern benches.

The Crisscross allows the leg vise to clamp your work without a parallel guide and pin. When I published the historical drawings for the X-shaped mechanism in 2007, I got letters from woodworkers who said it would never work. They had long explanations about force vectors and gravity. But they're wrong.

I found a historical example and bought it. I sent it to Benchcrafted to try out. They were the geniuses who made it. It's alien technology from the past, and I love it.

INTRODUCTION TO THE ANARCHIST'S WORKBENCH

The jaw of the chop (and front edge of the benchtop) are covered with a sheet of material made from chewed-up bits of cork and rubber. It's available at farm stores (and sold as gasket material) or you can get it from Benchcrafted under the brand name of Crubber.

The Crubber is about 1/8" thick, and I regularly get questions about why I glue a layer to the front edge of the benchtop. Doesn't this diminish the clamping capacity of the vise? Don't you want the work clamped to the entire front of the benchtop?

That was my concern 20 years ago as well, before I had built a bench. After working in the real world, I prefer the benchtop to be lined with grippy material. If you need support for a long workpiece, clamping it to the front of the benchtop (bending it 1/8") is no big deal.

If this concerns you, skip the grippy liner on the benchtop. Give it a try and see how you like it.

On the benchtop, the most essential piece of workholding is the blacksmith-made planing stop. It's a piece of iron embedded in a 2-1/2" x 2-1/2" x 12" stick of wood. The wood is friction fit in a through-mortise in the benchtop and moves up and down with mallet taps.

I've tried lots of planing stops – there are dozens of patented designs and manufactured versions, both vintage and new.

I prefer the old style, which goes back to the Romans (at least). It's a spike that is driven into a movable wooden part. On top of the spike is a flat area. That flat area has teeth (which hold your work) and is what gets hit by the mallet to move the stop down.

I definitely prefer this stop to the tricky commercial mechanisms that were made by Millers Falls and other companies, which have spring-loaded teeth and are locked with a screwdriver. This modern mechanism gets easily fouled and rusted. (And don't even get me started on the aluminum stops that open with a thumbscrew. My one-word tool review: Worthless.) Some modern makers have created a hybrid version that is bolted or screwed to the movable wooden post. These work great – I have no issue with them. I just like the old-school stops better.

Despite the safety concern of having the stop's teeth exposed, I'm going to be a bad boy. I didn't mortise the benchtop to receive the teeth of the planing stop. Two reasons:

I've never cut myself on it in 15 years of daily use.

THE ANARCHIST'S WORKBENCH

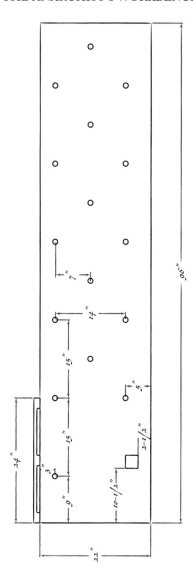

HOLDFAST HOLE PATTERN
This diagram shows the pattern of holdfast holes for the bench.

INTRODUCTION TO THE ANARCHIST'S WORKBENCH

I use the stop so much that the teeth are never down for more than a few moments.

Finally, there are the holdfast holes. I have spent more brainpower than I'd like to admit during the last 15 years trying to figure out the optimal pattern for holdfast holes. I sought a pattern that was useful but didn't make the benchtop look like a victim of the furniture beetle.

I think I have it right.

There is one holdfast hole behind the planing stop. This is used to secure a batten down across the width of the benchtop and against the planing stop – creating a wide planing stop for panels.

The remainder of the holdfast holes are in three rows on 15" centers. This accommodates the typical reach of a 7"-long holdfast pad (if you have radically smaller holdfasts, I encourage you to upgrade).

The back row is 3" from the back edge of the benchtop. You want it as far back as possible without cracking the benchtop – 3" is a workable and safe distance. The next two rows are 7" forward of the previous row. And each row is offset 7" or so down the length of the bench. You want the front row to end up about 5" from the front edge of the benchtop to hold appliances and workpieces.

This array of holes does everything I want. It holds boards of various widths with a doe's foot for planing. The row up near the front edge is ideal for securing a Moxon vise or any piece of work that needs to hang off the benchtop (think of a chair seat where you need to drill holes through the seat). I also have drilled three holes in the bench's right leg. These allow me to store holdfasts. While the holdfasts are stored, they sometimes act as a shelf and support long boards and doors.

Note that I use 1" holes for a holdfast. I have found that bigger holdfasts that are closely fit to their holes work better than small-diameter holdfasts with slop. If you can't find a 1" holdfast commercially, there are many blacksmiths who will make you one.

NO SLIDING DEADMAN

This bench does not have a sliding deadman, sometimes called a board jack. I don't think it needs one. If you take care when building your leg vise and add a grippy liner to its jaws, it will easily hold an 8'-long board for edge planing. Longer boards and doors can get some extra support from below using the holdfasts stored in the right leg.

If you think you need a deadman, know that they are an easy retrofit. Build the bench without one and use it. Your work and your preferences will tell you if it's a necessary piece of equipment.

THE SHELF

The shelf is not an afterthought. You need the shelf to hold the furniture parts you're working on, the jigs or appliances you use all the time and whatever else won't fit on your benchtop.

The shelf takes – at most – a couple hours to make, but it improves the bench forever. I've made the shelves in a variety of ways. Here are some pros and cons.

Cleats and loose boards without any edge joints. This is the fastest shelf imaginable. Screw some cleats to the stretchers. Then fill in the space with solid wood boards. The pros: Fast, and you can remove the shelf material to replace it. Cons: Gaps open when the boards shrink, and small stuff falls between the cracks. When you move the bench, the shelf boards spill everywhere.

Cleats and plain boards screwed or pegged in place. Pros: The shelf stays in one piece when you move it. Cons: You still get gaps when the shelf boards shrink.

Cleats and plywood screwed down or left loose. Pros: Fast and easy. Cons: Butt-ugly.

Cleats and shiplapped boards affixed with pegs or screws. Pros: When the shelf boards shrink, nothing falls through. Cons: Takes time to make the shiplaps. The seams fill with sawdust and crap.

Cleats with tongue-and-groove joints on the edges – affixed with pegs or screws. Pros: No unsightly gaps between the shelf boards. Most attractive solution. Cons: Most time-consuming, and the seams between the boards fill with sawdust.

I made my choices with this bench. The shelf boards are affixed to cleats using screws and have no shiplaps, tongues or grooves. There are six shelf boards that are 9" wide (allowing you to use up 2x10 material). And two are 2-1/2" wide (allowing you to use up scraps). I beveled the long edges of the shelf boards to make them more attractive. I'm OK with gaps opening up between the shelf boards. The sawdust ends up on the floor, where it's easy to sweep or vacuum.

INTRODUCTION TO THE ANARCHIST'S WORKBENCH

LUMBER MERCHANT, 'L'ART DU MENUISIER'
IF WOOD WAS EASILY AVAILABLE IN THE SAME DIMENSIONS AS IT WAS IN THE 18TH CENTURY, THIS WORKBENCH WOULD USE THICK, DRY STOCK.

PROS AND CONS OF THE BENCH

Here's what I like about this bench.

• Economy. It's cheap to build without compromises on weight, stiffness or strength. The material it's made from is plentiful, quickly renewed and costs pennies per pound.

• Flexibility. You can transform this bench into almost any sort of bench you want. Want to add a European tail vise? Then shift the benchtop to the right and do your business. Want to add a pattern-maker's vise? Shift the benchtop left and you'll have all the room you need. Those are radical changes that need to happen before construction begins. Most other changes are easy to make after the bench is built. You can add quick-release vises, a wagon vise or any surface vise with little fussing. You can even bolt a tool tray to the back edge of the benchtop. (I honestly don't mind.)

• Durability. Yellow pine gets tougher with age. The old yellow pine benches I have in my shop take an incredible beating and hold up as well as maple, and better than oak or cherry.

- Invisibility. I know, it's a weird word to describe a bench. This bench's simplicity makes clamping stuff to it a breeze. You can clamp stuff anywhere. There are no aprons, tool trays or vise mechanisms to stop you. It's difficult to describe how liberating this is until you are forced to use another bench that fights you every step of the way.

What about the cons? There are cons to every bench design, and I try to confront them head-on.

- Homely. The bench is not as attractive as the hardwood benches I've built. The contrast between the pale earlywood and dark orange latewood in yellow pine looks cheap. And the thin laminations for the components make the bench look more like a wooden countertop or bowling alley.
- Not ideal for fasteners. The softwood construction poses challenges when installing the leg vise hardware (which is covered in the building section). The bench doesn't use a lot of metal fasteners. But when you do use them (such as when bolting the seat to the leg), you need to use massive bolts.
- Vulnerability. Until the sap hardens, the wood is soft and easily dented. This might take a year or so.
- Thirsty for clamps. The top is laminated from lots of 1-1/4"-thick pieces. You'll need clamps, glue and patience to make a proper benchtop. Gluing up a top from thin strips of wood takes time, energy and clamps, clamps, clamps. But the result is (at the outset) more stable than a monolithic slab. (And you'll need those clamps for making furniture, too.)

A slab top would be faster to construct, but it has downsides. Thick slabs save you time when gluing up, but they're unstable for a few years until they settle down. They are more prone to splits and overall twisting than a laminated benchtop. Also, moving a wet slab can be difficult unless you own a forklift or have a lot of friends.

Same goes with the legs. The laminations are extra work, but that makes up for the fact that you don't have to find a sawmill that will mill up 5" x 5" sticks, which will take time to dry. And they might check or split.

INTRODUCTION TO THE ANARCHIST'S WORKBENCH

IN THE TRADITION

In the end, I consider this bench to be "traditional" in the best sense of the word. In many ways it is the same bench shown in A.J. Roubo's "l'Art du menuisier" from 1774 or the Hieronymus Wierix bench circa 1580. But it has been adapted – subtly – for its time and place. The vise hardware has been improved thanks to modern manufacturing techniques. And the raw materials reflect the reality that giant slabs of wood are now the exception rather than the rule.

The woodworkers of the 18th century had the same workholding goals as we do: To immobilize pieces of wood so we can easily work their faces, edges and ends. Wood hasn't changed much. The tools have changed only a little.

And above all else, I see this workbench simply as a tool for making furniture. It is not an expression of my mastery of the craft or my success at amassing capital.

That's where this bench comes from. And I suspect that most old workbenches came from the same place.

This bench is the result of a lot of listening to dead people. And now I hope to add a few words to that tradition.

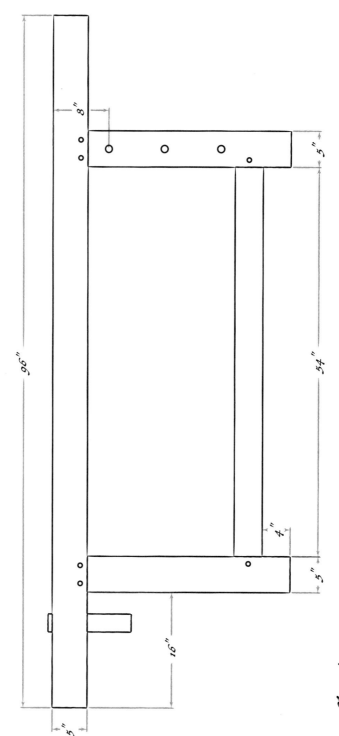

Elevation

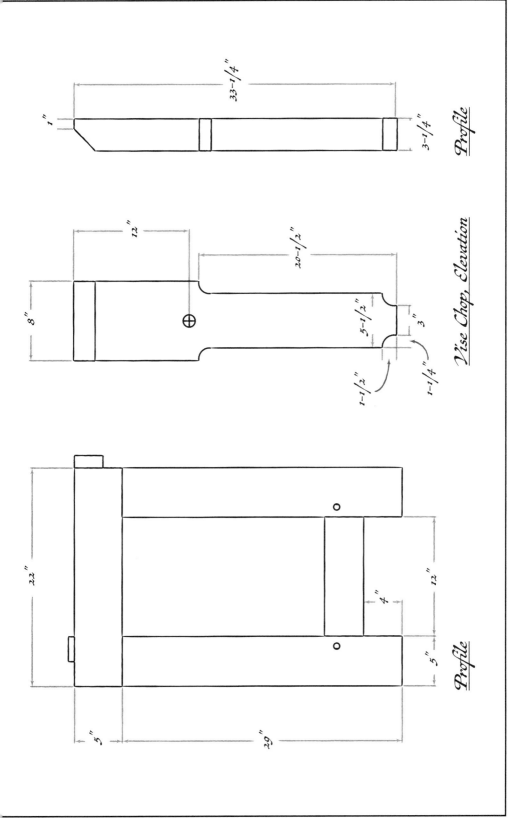

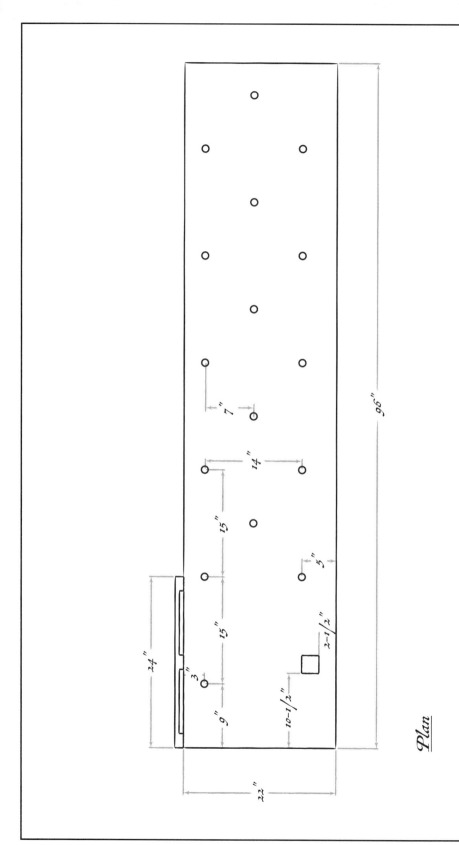

Plan

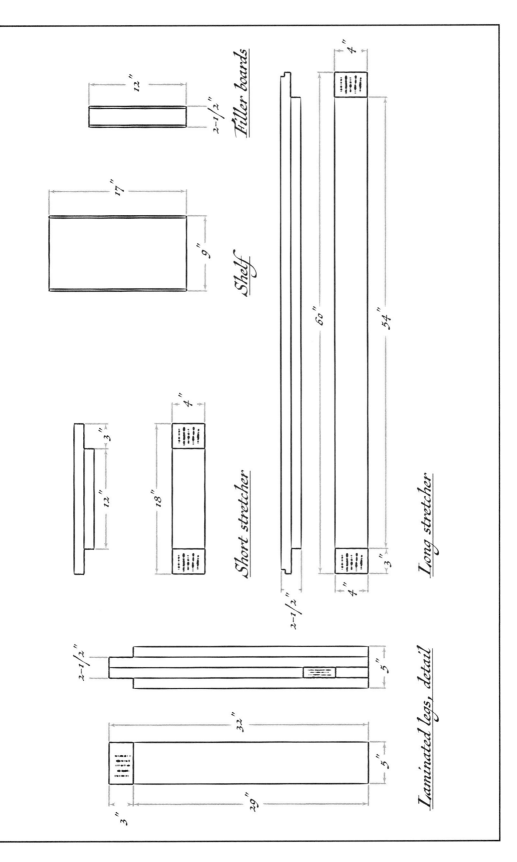

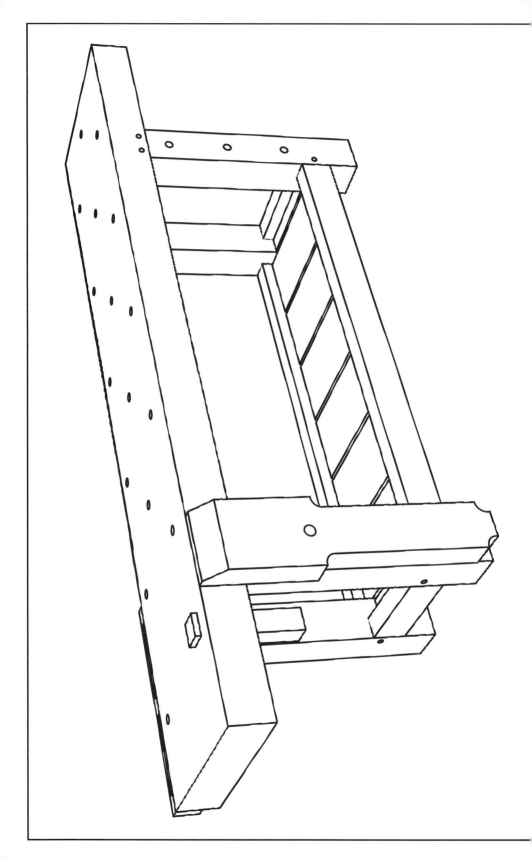

Cutting List: The Anarchist's Workbench

No.	Name	T.	W.	L.	Notes
1	Top	5	22	96	
4	Finished legs	5	5	32	Makes a 34" high bench
	8 Shoulder parts	1-1/4	5	29	
	8 Tenon parts	1-1/4	5	32	
2	Long stretchers	2-1/2	4	60	3" tenon, both ends
	2 Shoulder parts	1-1/4	4	54	
	2 Tenon parts	1-1/4	4	60	
2	Short stretchers	2-1/2	4	18	3" tenon, both ends
	2 Shoulder parts	1-1/4	4	12	
	2 Tenon parts	1-1/4	4	18	
6	Shelf boards	1-1/4	9	17	Bevel long edges
2	Shelf filler boards	1-1/4	2-1/2	12	Bevel long edges
2	Long cleats	1-1/4	1-1/4	54	
2	Short cleats	1-1/4	1-1/4	12	
1	Planing stop	2-1/2	2-1/2	12	
1	Vise jaw	3-1/4	8	35	Overlong, cut to fit

Shopping List

Benchtop: 9 @ 2x12x8'
Undercarriage: 3 @ 2x12x12' and 3 @ 2x10x10'

VINTAGE IRON BAR CLAMPS
WHEN GLUING UP LAMINATIONS WITH MULTIPLE LAYERS, HEAVY CLAMPS WITH A CRANK HANDLE ARE THE IDEAL TOOL.

CHAPTER XII
BUILD THE BENCHTOP

After trying it every which way, I think it's best to start building a workbench by first gluing up the benchtop. Then construct the base while working on that new benchtop. Put the two together, flip the thing over, sidestep any passing hernias and you have a workbench. The end.

I wrote the following chapters on the bench's construction assuming you have a basic knowledge of woodworking. You don't need to be an expert. But I hope you've made a couple items where you glued things together. Maybe you've made a rabbet, a tenon or dovetails. Bottom line: You have cut wood. And you have put pieces together. Right?

You don't need industrial machines to build this bench. Yes, you can build it entirely by hand. (I've built benches this way. And if you commit to the process, you can, too.) Most people will appreciate a few lightweight machines, which can turn a months-long process into about 40 or 50 hours of work. Here are the most important machines:

A 6" or 8" electric jointer. These sizes are entry-level machines and can serve you your whole life.

A 12" portable planer (also called a thicknesser). These inexpensive machines are magic.

A table saw. Any kind, small or large, will do.

A shed-load of clamps. To glue up all the laminations you need lots of clamps if you want tight joints. If you are cash-strapped, borrow clamps. If that's not an option, read on.

VINTAGE BAR CLAMPS

If you are poor, have no woodworking friends and want to build a workbench, you'll need to shop for vintage clamps. The world is filled with them. Heavy clamps in iron and steel have been manufactured for centuries, they almost never break and they are never thrown away. So haunt auctions (especially when workshops go out of business),

A CLAMP HEAD THAT WON'T SLIP
MODERN CLAMPS WITH A SLIDING CLUTCH WILL SLIP UNDER THE PRESSURE
YOU NEED TO GLUE UP A BENCHTOP. THESE WILL NOT.

garage sales and the occasional flea market.

You will find clamps.

Look for bar clamps that have two features: a sliding clamp head that is restrained by deep notches or detents in the clamp's bar (not just a friction clutch on a smooth bar). Plus a heavy Acme-thread screw driven by a cranked handle (that's better than a straight handle). Study the photos.

These two features ensure the clamp will apply an insane amount of pressure (almost too much pressure for woodworking, to be honest).

Most modern lightweight clamps apply pressure that is suitable for gluing furniture parts that are made well, fit tightly and don't need

BUILD THE BENCHTOP

much clamp pressure. The heavy bar clamps I'm describing for bench building are for tightening joints that other clamps can't touch.

I know that some virtue-signaling person in your past has told you that proper woodworking barely needs any clamps. Good joinery is enough. That's not true when building a bench. You'll be face-gluing six 1-1/2" x 5-1/2" x 96" pieces of yellow pine together in one go. You need clamps that can strangle the gaps between your boards.

Plus, once you get a taste for old iron clamps, you'll laugh at the plastic and aluminum ones on the market.

Expect to pay about $15 to $25 per clamp. That's a damn bargain, so don't whine about it. These clamps will last longer than most of your personal relationships. And they'll never make you cry. Until you drop one on your foot.

SORT YOUR WOOD

To make the benchtop you need nine 2x12x8' boards. You'll rip each one up the middle to make 18 sticks that measure 1-1/2" x 5-9/16" x 96". These 18 boards will make up your benchtop.

Ripping the 2x12s is a pain because some of your boards will be case hardened. They'll pinch the blade, or the two pieces will wander wildly as you rip them, causing havoc. When I encounter a case-hardened board, I stop the saw and lower the blade so it's cutting through only a little more than half the thickness of the board. I make that cut. Then I flip the board end-for-end and finish the cut. This usually works.

Sometimes you need to wedge open the kerf with wooden shims or a screwdriver as you make the cut.

Once you rip all the boards to width, joint and plane them to 1-1/4" thick. Arrange them on sawhorses or a table in a pleasing arrangement. Number their ends so you can keep all the parts under control. Scrawl a huge cabinetmaker's triangle on their edges. It's easy to get turned around when there's open glue in the room.

THE PLAN

I glue up a benchtop in three bundles of six boards. That's a lot of boards. And you might consider doing fewer boards (three, perhaps) until you hear the next thing I have to say: After you clamp up your boards, leave the chunk to cure overnight.

I know that's not what the glue bottle says. But here's the truth. Yel-

CAREFUL LAYOUT & LOTS OF MARKS WILL HELP
WHEN A GLUE BOTTLE IS OPEN, YOUR IQ DROPS 50 POINTS. NUMBER YOUR PARTS ON THE ENDS AND ADD A CABINETMAKER'S TRIANGLE ON THE BOARDS' EDGES TO KEEP EVERYTHING STRAIGHT.

low pine is packed with resin, and it's a dense wood. Those two things limit how easily the glue will penetrate the wood. You need all the help you can get.

After talking to a glue technologist at Franklin International, he recommended leaving a yellow pine bench lamination in the clamps for at least four hours. Overnight was better. (If you instead use an easily glued species, such as poplar, I'd clamp things for five hours total.)

Experience has proved him correct. When I let laminations sit overnight, they don't de-laminate. If I cheat, gaps might open in time. The top won't fall apart because of these gaps, but they are unsightly.

So if you need to leave each glue-up clamped up for 12 hours, do you really want to do 12 glue-ups? I don't. That's why I bundle my top pieces into six boards and make three glue-ups. Then I clean up these three laminations by running them through the planer. I edge joint them.

BUILD THE BENCHTOP

GAP IN LAMINATION, 2000-2020

This 1/16" gap opened up on my $175 Workbench after I built it. Filling it with epoxy and crap hasn't reduced my shame. The gap is the result of not leaving the lamination in the clamps long enough.

Then I glue the three 80-pound chunks into one benchtop. That's four glue-ups over four days. But I'm getting ahead of myself. Let's talk about doing your first glue up.

YELLOW GLUE

I use hide glue for most furniture making. But for workbenches I use yellow glue. Plain old polyvinyl acetate (type 1). Not the waterproof or water-resistant stuff (it's not necessary). Yellow glue is cheap, and you can buy it by the gallon (I forgot to mention that you'll probably need a gallon).

Lay out your pieces on your clamps. You want to roll on glue on two pieces and then fold the pieces together to slow the curing process. Then roll on glue on two more pieces.

You only need to put glue on one surface of each joint. Just use

ENOUGH GLUE FOR TWO
Glue one surface of the joint but use enough glue that both surfaces will be wetted. If you don't get any squeeze-out, then you were too stingy with the glue.

enough glue so that its mate will be wetted enough by the glue. Don't skimp. And using a little too much glue is better than using too little. Glue is cheap.

I roll it on with a cheap foam roller.

After you've glued all surfaces and piled the laminations together, apply clamp pressure. You should start from the middle. Clamp both above and below the laminations. I save the heavy iron clamps until the end for removing any gaps that my lightweight clamps cannot handle.

After the iron clamps are on, do not walk away. You'll regret it. In a large lamination, some of the clamps will loosen as the boards get closer together and the excess glue is squeezed out. Go back and tighten each clamp handle before you walk away.

BUILD THE BENCHTOP

PARALLEL-JAW CLAMPS ARE NOT ENOUGH
AFTER APPLYING YOUR REGULAR BAR CLAMPS, WHICH IMMOBILIZE THE PIECES, ADD THE HEAVY-DUTY IRON CLAMPS TO ELIMINATE GAPS.

ADD THE PLANING STOP

You can create the mortise for the 2-1/2" x 2-1/2" planing stop in the front lamination during glue-up, saving you some work later on. The mortise is located 11" from the end of the benchtop and is centered on the last lamination of six boards.

I'm sure it's obvious what we're going to do: Remove a 2-1/2"-long section from two laminations. To make life easier, we're going to insert a scrap 2-1/2" x 2" x 4" block into the mortise during glue-up to keep all the parts in line.

Here's how that works.

Cut the 2-1/2" out from the two center laminations using simple crosscuts. Then cut a 2-1/2" x 2" x 4" block of scrap wood. Drill pilot holes through it and nail it to one of the laminations next to the planing stop, 11" from the end.

Glue up the front lamination. About 30 minutes after you finish the

THE ANARCHIST'S WORKBENCH

CREATE A GAP FOR THE PLANING STOP
THIS BLOCK OF WOOD KEEPS THE FOUR LAMINATIONS IN LINE TO MAKE THE MORTISE FOR THE PLANING STOP. DRIVE THE NAILS IN ONLY A LITTLE – JUST ENOUGH TO HOLD THE BLOCK IN PLACE TEMPORARILY (ABOUT 1/4"). SNIP OFF THE NAIL HEADS IF THEY PROTRUDE FROM THE BLOCK.

final tightening of the clamps, use a block of wood and a small sledge to drive the spacer block out of its hole. Then clean up the mortise with a wet toothbrush and rags – get the glue out of the corners.

CLEANING UP

With any luck, the boards didn't slide up or down too much – I shoot for less than 1/16" variation across the entire bundle. Find a helper to joint and plane these bundles until they are smooth and square all around. It's quite difficult to do the job yourself and to do a good job.

After cleaning up the three laminations, check their long edges. Even if you did a good job on the machines, these edges can be angled or twisted. Before you try to glue up the entire benchtop, try to improve all the edges with handplanes (I use a jack and jointer). This is time well spent.

Show each edge to its mate. I had some gaps that were less than

BUILD THE BENCHTOP

REMOVE THE BLOCK
IF YOU DID IT RIGHT, THE BLOCK AND ITS NAILS WILL POP OUT OF THE MORTISE. IF THE NAILS STAYED IN THE BENCHTOP, YOU'LL NEED TO PRY THEM OUT.

THE ANARCHIST'S WORKBENCH

LAMINATE THE LAMINATIONS

After gluing up the three chunks, clean them up with handplanes or your machines. After you get the faces clean, joint the long edges with some assistance.

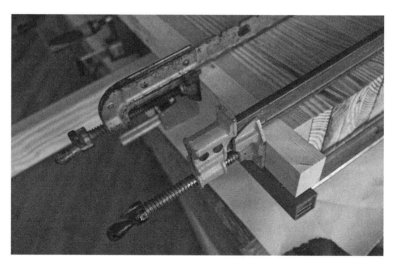

CLAMP PADS PROTECT FINISHED EDGES

I screwed these long clamp pads to the benchtop to keep them in place while applying clamp pressure. Having one less thing to worry about during glue-up is nice.

BUILD THE BENCHTOP

1/16" and I couldn't improve the fit with handplaning. Luckily, I found during a dry run that my clamps could eliminate those gaps.

Before you clamp up the top, make some clamping pads to protect the finished edges of the benchtop from being dented by the clamps. I ripped a 2x6 x 8' down its middle to make two 2"-wide x 8' pads. And I then screwed them to the ends of the benchtop (the screw holes will be cut away later).

Apply glue to the long edges of your parts. Begin by clamping below the benchtop. Then use your strong iron clamps to pull out any gaps that are visible on the top of the benchtop. Remove the glue squeeze-out with a wet rag to make your flattening chores easier later on.

The next day, flip the benchtop so it's upside down on sawhorses. Scrape off any excess glue. The underside should be pretty flat – less than 1/16" is what I shoot for with these big laminations. If it's out by a lot (1/8" or more) then you should flatten the underside with a jack plane before you start building the base.

THE ANARCHIST'S WORKBENCH

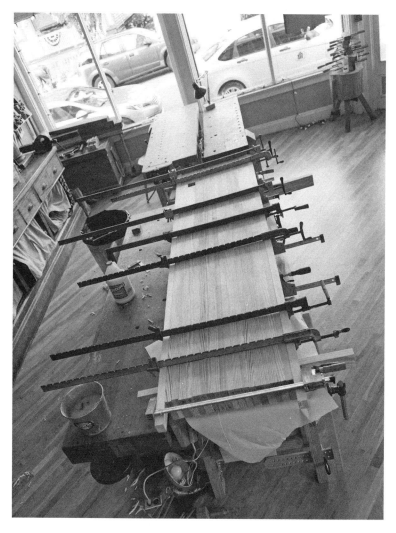

WALK AWAY
LET THE FINISHED BENCHTOP SIT OVERNIGHT IN THE CLAMPS. YOU SHOULD BE READY FOR A GOOD LONG SIT ANYWAY. TAKE IT.

BUILD THE BENCHTOP

COULDN'T HELP IT
The underside was out by 1/16", but I decided to true it up anyway. I love the texture of a surface that has been traversed with a jack plane. It looks tidy. And it takes about 10 minutes.

FINESSE IS REQUIRED, EVEN WITH LARGE PARTS
WHEN WORKING WITH LARGE COMPONENTS MADE WITH CONSTRUCTION LUMBER, IT'S EASY TO FORGET THAT GOOD WORK IS IMPORTANT.

CHAPTER XIII
BUILD THE BASE

The parts for the workbench's base are created by laminating lots of 1-1/4"-thick bits of pine together. The laminations are also used to create much of the joinery for the base. Using notches and plywood spacers as you glue things up, you'll make all eight tenons required for the bench, plus four of the 12 mortises you need.

It's easy to do if you make all your pine parts exactly the same 1-1/4" thickness. I'm repeating the 1-1/4" stuff for emphasis, another mark of quality literature.

PROCESSING THE STOCK

Rip all the stock using the techniques described earlier to avoid case-hardening woes. Rip the parts about 1/4" over-wide compared to the cutting list. Crosscut all your parts 2" overlong compared to the cutting list. It might seem wasteful, but creating slightly oversized parts gives you flexibility to deal with defects. And it gives you some breathing room as you work to your target width and thickness.

Plane everything down to 1-1/4" in one session. Don't run a few parts then come back later and run some more. If everything is the exact same thickness, assembly will be easy (well, easier).

With the stock planed down, begin by making the legs.

LORD OF THE RINGS

The first thing to do is arrange the four boards that will make up each leg of the bench. You're going to look at these legs for decades, so arrange the grain and color on the edges so things don't look stupidly jarring. Hide knots and defects.

But wait, there's one other important consideration. When gluing up boards face-to-face, try to orient the growth rings sympathetically in each leg. What the hell does that last sentence even mean? Basically, the heart side of one board should always touch the bark side of its neighbor. A photo explains it easily.

WRONG & RIGHT
ON THE LEFT, THE PARTS AREN'T ARRANGED IDEALLY. THAT TOP BOARD SHOULD BE FLIPPED 180°. ON THE RIGHT IS A LEG THAT IS GLUED UP IDEALLY.

Why? If the boards in the lamination cup, they will help keep the seams at the edges closed and tight. Why, again? Remember: The bark side of a board becomes cupped as it dries. The heart side bows out. Put a bow and a cup together and the shapes are sympathetic or complementary. Put a bow against a bow (or a cup against a cup) and you might have a struggle on your hands (or some gaps at the seams).

CREATE THE TENONS & MORTISES

Once you have the leg pieces arranged properly, crosscut the four leg laminations to final length. The two interior laminations are 3" longer than the two exterior laminations. That creates the tenon that goes into the benchtop.

Once you get the leg stock crosscut, you can cut notches that will create the mortises for the long stretchers.

First, decide the position of each leg – front, back, left, right – and draw a cabinetmaker's triangle on the top of the leg parts to keep them

BUILD THE BASE

CUT NOTCHES TO MAKE FAST MORTISES
After crosscutting the top and bottom of the mortise, chop out the waste with a chisel. Strike blows from both faces, and the waste will fall away easily.

INSTANT SHOULDERS & CHEEKS
The scrap keeps the laminations from sliding around. This creates a perfect tenon after assembly.

BEFORE THE PANIC
THIS IS WHAT MY LEG LAMINATIONS LOOK LIKE BEFORE I WARILY POP THE TOP OFF THE GLUE BOTTLE.

oriented. That will help you figure out where the mortises should be.

The mortises are 4" up from the floor. And they are 1-1/4" x 4" x 3-1/8" deep. So basically, you have to cut a 4" x 3-1/8" notch in one lamination of each leg. When you glue up the leg, the notch becomes a mortise.

Saw two walls of the notch and pop out the waste with a chisel. It's quick work.

Before you glue up the leg, you can make things easier by nailing on some scraps of wood to keep the outer laminations in place. Cut some scrap plywood to 3" long by the width of the leg pieces (about 5-1/4"). Nail the scraps in place.

With the leg laminations loosely put together, mark the mortise location on the neighboring laminations. Then tape off those areas so they won't get glue on them during assembly.

BUILD THE BASE

NAILS HELP THE CLAMPS
A couple skinny nails through the laminations makes the glue-up much easier. Put the nails where they will do no harm. (It would be bad to put nails where the drawbore pegs or vise screw might go.)

Gluing up the legs is a lot like gluing up the top – lots of glue applied with a roller. The difference here is that I also nail the laminations together, layer by layer, so they don't slide around. The nail isn't a fastener – it adds no strength – but it keeps your parts from shifting when they shouldn't.

First apply glue and put one outer lamination against one inner lamination. Drive a couple nails through the inner lamination and into the outer (this way no one will see the nail heads). Then add another inner lamination – and a couple nails. The last outer lamination can be nailed in place, but the nail heads will show. I usually skip the nails here, figuring I can prevent one lamination from sliding around too much.

Clamp up the laminations. Look for gaps. Remove the excess squeeze-out. Look for gaps all around. Tighten the clamps again. Look for gaps. Remove any more squeeze-out. Look for gaps.

You'll also want to carefully check all the seams for gaps.

Let the leg sit in the clamps overnight. Repeat this process for the other three legs. After you remove the clamps, pop the scraps off the tenons. I use a pry bar. And peel the tape off the mortise walls.

Gluing up the stretchers is easier than the legs. There are only two laminations. There are no mortises. And the scraps that make the tenons help keep things from sliding.

Crosscut your pieces to size. The inner lamination is 6" longer than the outer lamination. That means each tenon will be 1-1/4" x 4" wide x 3" long. So cut some plywood scraps so they are 4" wide x 3" long and nail them to the ends of the long laminations.

Glue and clamp up each lamination, just like you did for the legs. Tighten the clamps, remove excess glue and look for gaps. You know the routine.

MORTISES FOR THE SHORT STRETCHERS

Once everything is out of the clamps, you still need to cut four mortises in the legs to receive the short stretchers. These mortises are the same size as the other mortises – 1-1/4" x 4" x 3-1/8" deep. With mortises this big, it's best to bore out most of the waste and finish the job with a chisel.

First lay out the locations of the four mortises. They are 4" up from the floor, and so you'll quickly realize that the two mortises in each leg

BUILD THE BASE

SURROUNDING THE SHOULDERS
NAIL THE SCRAPS IN PLACE, BUTTED AGAINST THE FRONT LAMINATION OF THE STRETCHER. THE FRONT LAMINATION SHOULD BE A SNUG FIT BETWEEN THE TWO SCRAPS.

DRILL, THEN OVERLAP
Drill out the extents of the mortise. Then come back and drill out the middle part. Overlap the holes over and over until you get a pill-shaped mortise. Chisels finish the job.

will intersect. That's fine and we'll rabbet the tenons to make everything fit like a puzzle inside.

After laying out the mortises (I do it with marking gauges and knives), drill out the waste. I used a 1-1/4" Forstner bit in a drill press. If you don't have a drill press, use an electric drill or a brace and drill 1"- or 1-1/8"-diameter holes.

Now square up the corners of the mortise with a chisel and a mallet. For years – years – I used a corner chisel to do this operation. It seemed the smart thing to do. Need to square a corner? How about a corner chisel?

I don't own a corner chisel anymore – they don't do a better job and they are a pain to sharpen. Just knock the waste out with a simple bevel-edge chisel and a mallet. First, I bust up the waste with the chisel oriented perpendicular to the grain of the junk in the corner. Then I remove the waste with the chisel's edge parallel to the grain. By the

BUILD THE BASE

CLEAR THE CORNERS

It's short work to square up the corners with a chisel and a mallet. Check your work as you get deep into the mortise to make sure the tool isn't drifting.

MEASURE THE GAP
Drive one tenon into a leg. Then drive the other tenon in. It will come to a stop before its shoulder contacts the leg. Measure this gap (it should be 1/2" or close). That's the size of the rabbet you need to make on the backside of the tenon.

fourth mortise, you'll be an expert. And you'll be done.

FIT THE TENONS

Plane the machine marks off the stretchers and fit the tenons to their mortises. Try to do as much work on the tenon as you can (it's easier to manipulate the tenons than the interior of the mortise). But you probably will have to chisel out bits of the mortise to get things to work.

I strive to be able to sink each tenon with hand pressure alone. If I have to mallet it home, it's too tight. If the tenon enters in the mortise like a mouse in Mammoth Cave, it's too loose (glue some thin scraps on the tenon to tighten up the fit, or drawbore the joint and try not to worry so much).

BUILD THE BASE

STEPS TO A GOOD FIT
The rabbet on the backside of the tenon allows it to fit against its mate inside the leg. Saw out the rabbet. Adjust its fit, if necessary, with a chisel or shoulder plane.

INSIDE THE LEG
This is how the two tenons should nest together. There's lots of strength, thanks to the tight fit and square shoulders.

After you get all the tenons going into their respective mortises, you will notice a problem. The two tenons in each leg intersect in the middle of the mortise – tip to tip. One traditional way to fix this is to miter the ends of both tenons. I've done this many times. At some point I started rabbeting one end of one tenon instead, which seemed easier to my miter-dodging mind.

On paper, the rabbet should be 1/2" x 1/2", but you should confirm this by putting the two tenons in the mortise and measuring how much meat needs to be butchered away.

You can make the rabbets on either the long stretchers or the short. Cut the rabbet with a handsaw, which is the most direct, non-stupid way to accomplish this simple task. Make sure the two tenons nest together nicely in their shared mortise.

DRAWBORING

With all the legs and stretchers apart, now is the time to drill the holes for the drawboring. Why now? Because you will use the drawbore pegs to temporarily cinch the base tight while marking out the mortises on the underside of the benchtop.

First mark out where the 5/8" holes for the pegs should go on the legs. All the centers should be 1" away from the long edge of the leg – any closer and you risk splintering the leg. And if you move it too far toward the end of the tenon, you will destroy the tenon when you drive the peg home.

For the long stretchers, I centered the holes on the 4" mortise opening. For the short stretchers, I moved the center point up 7/8" so that the two holes didn't intersect in the middle of the leg. That is bad, and I have done it.

Drill the holes all the way through the leg. They are not blind holes.

Now you need to drill the holes through the tenons. These are offset 1/8" toward each tenon's shoulder. Toward the tenon shoulder. Toward. You will do this wrong at some point in your life. Try to save that mistake for a future project.

Put each joint together. Then take a 5/8" Forstner or auger bit and drive it into the 5/8" hole to mark the center point on the tenon cheek. Disassemble the joint and then move the center point 1/8" toward the tenon shoulder. Toward. Then drill a 5/8" hole through each tenon.

BUILD THE BASE

OFFSET BORES
Here you can see how the holes don't intersect. The offset holes avoid some dramatic failures at assembly time.

MARK THE CENTER POINT
The tip of a Forstner bit makes a nice sharp mark on the tenon cheek. I like to knock the bit into the hole with a mallet to ensure the mark is crisp and deep.

MOVE THE CENTER

I DRAW A LINE THROUGH THE CENTER POINT TO ENSURE I MOVE THE LOCATION OF MY HOLE SO IT'S PARALLEL TO THE LONG EDGES OF THE TENON AND NOT JUST FOLLOWING SOME GRAIN LINE (YOU'LL KNOW WHEN YOU MAKE THIS MISTAKE). MARK THE NEW LOCATION OF THE CENTER POINT SO IT'S 1/8" TOWARD THE SHOULDER.

MAKE YOUR PEGS

I make my drawbore pegs using 5/8" x 5" dowel I've shaved from straight-grained material (yes you can buy the stuff from the store; just look for poker-straight grain). Then I point one end of each peg like a pencil, about 1-1/2" from the end. Apply candle wax (paraffin) to the whole peg. This will make the peg go in easily (and go out when you are temporarily assembling the base).

Turn the benchtop so it's upside down on your sawhorses. Assemble the bench's base loosely on the underside of the benchtop so it's also upside down. Tap the drawbore pegs a bit into each hole. As soon as the joint tightens up, stop with the taps.

BUILD THE BASE

WAX IS YOUR FRIEND

I learned this from an Alaskan timber framer. Wax your drawbore pegs instead of gluing them. Glue makes a peg swell up. Wax helps a peg do its job, which is to slide into place.

DRIVING THE DRAWBORE PEGS HOME
The bench is assembled without clamps. Straight-grained oak pegs pull the joints tight.

CHAPTER XIV
ASSEMBLY & VISES

Getting the eight joints in the workbench's base to fit together is one thing. Adding four more joints so the benchtop and base dock together nicely requires careful layout, accurate mortising and (if you aren't careful) straining your body like you just ate six cheese pizzas.

Each leg weighs about 20 lbs. and can easily wedge fast into its mortise as you fit the joint. Remember: Don't drive the legs in with a mallet (or a sledge). As a timber framer once said: "You should be able to sink a tenon using your hat." The real strength in the joints comes from the mechanical lock of the drawbore pegs.

After I built a few benches this way, I understood why many people skip this step, joining the base to the benchtop with fasteners or loose dowels instead. It is, however, worth the effort to do it the hard way. Drawboring the base into the benchtop adds a layer of solidity you can feel as you work.

LAY OUT THE MORTISES

With the bench base dry-assembled and upside down on the benchtop, place the tenons on the legs where they need to go on the benchtop. You don't have to be persnickety (yet). Trace the locations of the tenons on the benchtop with a pencil. Now shift the base to the side.

Place a layer of masking tape over your pencil lines, making sure you have (at least) 1/4" of tape outside your pencil lines. Now comes the fussy part. You're going to put the base in its final position, trace around the tenons with a knife edge – slicing through the tape. Then you'll peel away the interior section of tape and know the exact boundaries of your mortises.

This is a common trick when dovetailing (all thanks to Mike Pekovich for sharing it with the world). It works for lots of other joints, too.

Place the base in position and center it on the benchtop, left-to-right. The front legs and the front edge of the benchtop should be in

TAPE THE JOINT
Usually I mark the joints out with a knife line and a pencil, but using blue tape makes it a little easier. Here I've covered the areas for the mortises with one layer of tape.

the same plane. Now check your work with a square and tape measure.

Are the legs perfectly perpendicular to the benchtop? If not, add some clamps to the base to pull the legs into position.

Are the legs the same distance apart at the floor as they are at the benchtop? If not, you can use a spreader clamp or regular bar clamp to pull the legs into position. In extreme cases, I'll clamp a block between the legs that's equal to the shoulder-to-shoulder length of the stretcher. This pulls the legs parallel to their neighbors.

To mark the joints, remove the cutter from a block plane. Use a corner of the blade like a knife to trace the shape of the tenons on the tape. The wide, flat back – and lack of a handle – make it an ideal tool for the job. A stroke or two should slice through the tape. Then remove the base from the benchtop. Peel away the tape that was touching the tenons. Now you have your target.

DRILL OUT THE MORTISES

I drill out the majority of the waste with an auger then remove the remainder with a heavy chisel. The hard part of this job is keeping

ASSEMBLY & VISES

AN ODD KNIFE

A BLOCK PLANE BLADE MAKES SHORT WORK OF TRACING THE SHAPE OF THE TENON ONTO THE BENCHTOP FOR THE MORTISE. YOU HAVE TO ANGLE THE BLADE QUITE A BIT WHEN MARKING THE TENON'S FACE CHEEKS, BUT IT WORKS.

PEEL AWAY THE MORTISE

AS YOU REMOVE THE TAPE FROM THE BENCHTOP, A MARKING KNIFE HELPS SLICE THROUGH THE TAPE IN PLACES YOU MIGHT HAVE MISSED WITH THE BLOCK PLANE BLADE.

SIMPLE DRILLING GUIDE
HERE I HAVE MY BIT IN A CORNER CREATED BY TWO WALLS. IF YOU OBSERVE THE BIT AS YOU WORK AND DRILL AT A SLOW SPEED, YOU'LL GET GOOD RESULTS.

your chisel on track as you chop and pare the mortise walls.

I always build a one-time-use jig that helps keep my auger bit dead perpendicular to the benchtop. This makes the chisel work easier. And it helps keep me in the lines.

The jig is four pieces of plywood screwed together. See the photo above. There aren't any critical dimensions except for the height of the "walls" of the jig. That dimension depends on the length of your auger bit. You want to make the walls tall enough to help guide the auger bit, but not so tall that the drill's chuck hits them.

Chuck your auger in the drill and measure how much of the bit extends, from the bit's cutting flutes to the jaws of the chuck. With my bit, that measurement is 6". I want to drill about 3-1/8" deep into the benchtop. That extra 1/8" gives me room for any excess glue or bits of wood at the bottom of the mortise. So I ripped my jig's walls to be 2-7/8" wide.

That means as soon as the jaws of the drill line up with the walls I

RESULTS

CAREFUL SPACING OF YOUR HOLES ALLOWS YOU TO GET MOST OF THE MORTISE'S PERIMETER DRILLED OUT. THE CENTER CHUNK OF WOOD CAN BE PRIED OUT WITH A CHISEL.

can stop drilling. It's not a depth stop, more of a depth suggestion. A depth thought? A depth opinion? Bah, I need to work on that joke.

Once you make the jig it will become obvious how to use it. The two 90° inside corners are ideal for drilling out the matching corners of the mortises. Place the jig so the walls just cover the masking tape. Clamp the jig down. Drill a hole. You can use other parts of the jig's wall to drill out sections of the mortise that don't have to be perfectly perpendicular.

(Oh hey, if you are an engineer, you can stop writing that note to me about how to improve my jig. Yes, I could build it so there are four inside corners that exactly match the size of the mortise. But this jig took me three minutes to make and required no persnickety measuring. But do what you need to do to make yourself happy.)

One word of advice about using the jig: Don't run your drill at full speed. A fast-moving auger will throw around chips with a lot of force. The flying hot waste (hmmm, not a bad band name) will jerk the jig out

ACCURATE SITTING

I AM PERCHED TO THE SIDE OF THE CHISEL, SIGHTING THE BACK OF THE TOOL AGAINST THE BENCHTOP. I MAKE SMALL ADJUSTMENTS AFTER EACH MALLET STRIKE TO RETURN IT TO DEAD PLUMB.

ASSEMBLY & VISES

JACK THE CHEEK
A FEW SWIPES ON THE EDGE CHEEKS HELP YOU FIT THE TENON WITHOUT REQUIRING YOU TO PLANE THE WHOLE DAMN LEG FOR 20 MINUTES. YOU CAN SEE WHERE THE STROKE STARTED RIGHT WHERE THE TENON'S SHOULDER BEGINS.

of position. If you take it slowly (I pull the trigger about half speed), the chips won't dislodge the jig. As you've probably figured out, this is my voice of shame typing this entire paragraph.

CHISEL THE WASTE

The rest of the job is accurate, unrequited bashing. Removing waste from deep mortises is all about steering the chisel so it remains perpendicular to the benchtop. This is all about where you are sitting and where you are looking. If you cannot see if the chisel's back is 90° to the benchtop then you are beating it blind.

Put another way: If you are looking at the front or back face of the chisel as you work, you're blind. You need to be to the side of your chisel. And if you are new to this operation, I recommend a small try square back there to help guide your eye.

Whacking the ends of the mortises is obviously more work than

CHEAT AT DRAWBORING

Traditionally, a drawbore pin is used to deform the hole through the tenon to provide an easy path for the peg at assembly. If you don't have a large enough drawbore pin (I couldn't find mine), you can accomplish the same thing with a tapered reamer.

peeling off the long walls of the mortise, which are parallel to the grain. But the tendency is to make the same error: either the chisel is leaning too far forward or too far back.

FIT THE TENONS

Even with careful layout and chopping, the tenons are likely to be too tight. My first strategy is to plane the faces of the legs to remove any machine marks. You have to do this anyway, and it will help fit the edge cheeks (because there is no shoulder).

Then, for extra measure, I use a coarse-set jack plane to remove a little more from the tenons' edge cheeks. This is usually about four strokes on each cheek. If you start your plane in the right place, the marks won't be noticeable.

You also need to remove some wood from the face cheeks. The best way to do this is with a wide shoulder plane. But a chisel can do the job (as can several other tools). Take a few strokes from each cheek. Then try the tenon in its mortise.

As I said at the beginning of this chapter, these tenons should slide right in. No malleting.

You might need to remove some waste in the mortise, especially if the tenon ends up sitting cock-eyed in its mortise.

DRAWBORE THE TENONS

The legs are drawbored into the benchtop in the same manner as you drawbored the stretchers. Each tenon receives two 5/8" pegs. The holes are 1" from the underside of the benchtop and are 1-1/4" from the extents of the mortise.

With the tenon removed, drill the 5/8" holes into the benchtop, passing through the open mortise. Bottom out the bit in the hole (mine went 6" into the benchtop). Place the tenon in its mortise, mark the location of the holes using your auger bit. Remove the leg and shift the center point 1/8" toward the shoulder.

Drill the 5/8" holes in the tenons using that new mark.

Now put the tenon back in its mortise and check your work. If the offset between the two holes seems too heavy, I use a tapered reamer to open up the hole through the tenon. This creates a nice "on ramp" through the tenon so the peg doesn't shatter when you drive it in.

Make your pegs from 5/8" oak dowels cut 7" long. Taper one end of

NOT FOR CLAMPING
THE BACK EDGE OF THE BENCHTOP DOESN'T NEED TO BE COPLANAR TO THE BACK OF THE LEGS. IT'S NOT A CLAMPING SURFACE. IF YOU ARE OCD, RESIST THE TEMPTATION TO PLANE THINGS FLUSH. YOU MIGHT NEED THAT EXTRA LITTLE BIT OF BENCHTOP WIDTH SOMEDAY.

each peg like a pencil. You can taper up to about 2" of each peg's length without reducing the hold of the peg. Wax the pegs and disassemble the bench. Plane up the front edge of the benchtop. Don't worry about the back edge. In fact, on my bench the legs aren't flush to the back edge of the benchtop.

TRUE THE ENDS OF THE BENCHTOP

At some point you will need to trim the ends of the benchtop. Now is as good a time as any with the benchtop upside down on sawbenches. Lay out the lines using a framing square. I use a simple circular saw and make the cut in several passes (otherwise the saw's blade will deflect).

You'll finish the job by sawing from the top of the benchtop. And if

ASSEMBLY & VISES

TRIM FROM BELOW
Cut the benchtop to length with a circular saw. Begin on the underside. Then flip the top over and finish the job.

CHISEL THE REMAINING WASTE
Chop out any excess waste from sawing the ends to length. Then remove the last bit of waste with a wide chisel.

THE ANARCHIST'S WORKBENCH

FOLLOW THE INSTRUCTIONS
Follow the instructions, except where I tell you not to. One more word of advice, do not rush or take shortcuts. Installing vise hardware is best done methodically.

you own a standard circular saw, you'll still have waste to remove after cutting from both faces. I finished the job with a handsaw. Even if you are a good sawyer, you will have chunks of waste to remove. I chopped them away with a chisel. It's much like chopping away waste between dovetails.

After chopping the waste to a thin ribbon (see photo on the previous page), I removed the last bit of waste with a wide chisel, working from the ends toward the center of the benchtop. Then I planed the ends flat. Which sucked.

At this point it's best to install any vise hardware that requires holes, grooves or mortises in the legs. It's easier when the parts are apart.

START THE LEG VISE

Again, this is the point where I sympathize with people who simply bolt a quick-release face vise to the benchtop and call it a done bench. Leg vises require some precision boring. And they require a mortise or

ASSEMBLY & VISES

CHEAP SUBSTITUTE
Using No. 14 screws increased the price of the bench by less than $1. I used No. 14 x 1-1/2" screws into the jaw. And No. 14 x 2" screws into the leg. I drilled a 5/32" pilot for each screw and drove them in by hand.

some grooves for the hardware that makes the jaw cinch down hard.

I do, however, think leg vises are worth the fuss.

The first step is to make the jaw, sometimes called the "chop." I make mine from maple, though yellow pine will do fine. (I prefer maple for a reason I cannot put into words.) To create the jaw, I laminate two lengths of 8/4 maple face-to-face. By the time the jaw is glued up and squared up, it's usually about 3-1/4" thick.

After the glue is dry, square up the jaw and follow the instructions for your bench hardware. I think it's a waste of ink to repeat the instructions here, so I'm going to explain only where I did things differently. The first place I go off the map is when attaching the Crisscross mechanism to the leg and jaw. The instructions have you tap the wood then use machine screws to attach the hardware. I use wood screws instead.

Why? Softwoods such as yellow pine do not tap well. At all. I've tried it with denser yellow pines and cottonwood. In all cases the

TENON SURGERY
YOU NEED TO SAW AWAY A SMALL BIT OF THE TENON SO THE CRISSCROSS HARDWARE WILL FUNCTION. MARK OUT WHAT YOU NEED TO REMOVE AND SAW IT AWAY.

threads strip out after a short period of time. So I switched to No. 14 wood screws. The other advantage to using screws is you don't need to buy a tap and die.

The other complication you will encounter when installing Crisscross hardware is how the tenon for the front stretcher of the base intersects the groove for the hardware. You need to remove a little chunk of the tenon. It's not a big deal, and the path you need to take will be obvious once you get to this point. I marked out the chunk I needed to remove and cut it away with a handsaw.

After the vise hardware is installed and running smoothly in the leg, remove it all and assemble the bench.

ASSEMBLY

I assemble the bench using liquid hide glue because it has a long open time, it is easily cleaned with hot water (even after it has set up) and it's reversible if things go incredibly awry. I don't use bar clamps.

ASSEMBLY & VISES

BEGIN AT THE END
START WITH THE END. GLUE UP THE ENDS AND KNOCK THE DRAWBORE PEGS IN JUST A LITTLE SO THE STRETCHER WON'T FALL OUT.

And the glue is just extra insurance because the drawbore pegs provide all the pressure you need.

Assemble the bench upside down on sawhorses. First glue the ends of the bench base together and knock the drawbore pegs in a little to hold things together. Don't drive any pegs home until the entire bench is together.

After you get the end assemblies together, put the long stretchers in place in one of the end assemblies. Knock in the pegs a little. Add the other end assembly and its pegs. Then put the assembled base into its mortises in the benchtop. Add the drawbore pegs. Then knock everything home.

FINISH THE WORKHOLDING

After the bench is assembled, re-attach the vise hardware. Now is a good time to install any lining to the jaw and the bench. You can use suede or a cork/rubber composite material sold at farm supply stores

ADD THE LONG STRETCHERS
Same deal. Slide them in place. Knock in their pegs.

ASSEMBLY & VISES

JOIN THE ENDS
Knock the other end onto the tenons on the long stretchers. Add the drawbore pegs.

THE ANARCHIST'S WORKBENCH

DRIVE THE PEGS

Start with the pegs for the top. Then the long stretchers. Then the short stretchers. This procedure will shift any unsightly gaps to the short stretchers. And then you are done. Saw off any protruding pegs. Plane them clean and flush.

ASSEMBLY & VISES

ADD THE LINER
HERE YOU CAN SEE THE LINERS, THE PLYWOOD CAUL AND THE WAX PAPER. IN ADDITION TO CLAMPING THINGS IN PLACE WITH THE VISE SCREW, I ALSO ADD A COUPLE BAR CLAMPS.

for making gaskets. Benchcrafted, which makes this leg vise, sells it under the brand name of "Crubber."

Sticking the liner to the jaw and benchtop is simple work (oh no, more laminating). Apply glue to the liner, tape it in position, then close the vise. I add a piece of plywood covered in wax paper in between as a clamping caul. This helps distribute the clamping pressure. Also, the wax paper prevents the glue from sticking where it shouldn't.

But which glue? I prefer epoxy. It's expensive and it stinks, but I have found it to be the most reliable in the long term.

Once the vise is complete, you can install the planing stop. It's a piece of yellow pine that is 2-1/2" x 2-1/2" x 12. You'll have to laminate two layers of 2x material to make the stop. I recommend you laminate a backup piece because some people split their first planing stop.

Plane up the stick until it fits in its mortise in the benchtop and moves with sharp mallet blows.

THE ANARCHIST'S WORKBENCH

HOW TIGHT?
MY PLANING STOPS MOVE ABOUT 1/8" WHEN I STRIKE THEM. THAT'S THE SWEET SPOT (FOR ME). IF THEY ARE TIGHTER, THAT'S TEDIUM. LOOSER? YOUR STOP WILL FLY OUT OF ITS MORTISE ONE DAY.

After I fit the wooden part of the stop, I install the iron hook. Mine was made by blacksmith Tom Latane. There are lots of ways to install these. Here's how I do it.

I drill a stepped hole. The diameters of the holes are determined by measuring the shaft of the hook at three places. The tip. The midpoint. And right under the hook. I make the measurement from corner to corner with calipers.

For this stop, the tip measured .35". The middle was .56". And the top was .60". The shaft was 4-1/4" long. So I first drilled a 5/8" hole (.625" in diameter) 2" into the planing stop. Then I drilled a 3/8" hole as deep as the bit would go (about 4-1/2").

When I slipped the planing stop's shaft in the hole (…must resist… the jokes are too easy) it stopped about two-thirds of the way in. Then I tapped it in place the rest of the way. If things seem too loose (or the stop comes out at some point) slather it with epoxy and drive it back in.

ASSEMBLY & VISES

FIRST OF MANY TAPS
Light taps should seat the shaft, especially in yellow pine. If your stop is oak, it will require heavier strikes.

DRILLING GUIDE
I'VE MADE MANY KINDS OF JIGS FOR DRILLING HOLDFAST HOLES, INCLUDING SOME THAT WORKED LIKE A GIANT DOWELING JIG. THIS, HOWEVER, IS MY FAVORITE WAY TO DO THIS TASK. IT'S NOT FUSSY AND DOES A GOOD JOB.

If the planing stop splits as you tap it in, make a new one and drill slightly wider holes.

HOLDFAST HOLES

The third important workholding device in this workbench is the holdfast with its array of holes in the benchtop (and the front leg). Holdfasts do things that bar clamps cannot. They hold your work and appliances in places that a bar clamp simply cannot reach.

While most woodworkers understand how holdfasts function, they struggle with where to put the holes. Or they flat-out resist drilling the holes through their beautifully laminated benchtop.

I think it's like skydiving or pulling the bandage off an old wound. The anticipation is excruciating. The relief on the other side is eye-opening. Do your best not to hesitate, fret or think too much.

ASSEMBLY & VISES

Because after you start using holdfasts you'll wonder how you got along without them.

I have studied lots of old benches and experimented with different hole patterns, gradually adding more holes until I saw a useful pattern emerge. I now use three rows of holdfasts that are staggered. The holes in each row are spaced apart based on the reach of the holdfast. My holdfasts reach 8", so the holes are on 15" centers. The rows are 7" away from the next row, also to accommodate the reach of the tool.

This allows me to clamp battens or a doe's foot (a notched batten) just about anywhere on the bench. I can secure a Moxon vise at the front edge of the benchtop. I can also secure sticking boards, shooting boards and bench hooks.

I also have one additional holdfast hole behind the metal planing stop. This hole helps secure a wide planing stop across the width of the benchtop.

The hole layout in the construction drawings shows the pattern.

I prefer 1" holdfast holes, which is a more traditional size to the modern 3/4" standard. This requires a heavier holdfast with a shaft just under 1" in diameter. The closer the fit between the shaft and its hole, the better the holdfast will do its job.

Also important: The hole must be perpendicular to the benchtop or the holdfast will not work in some instances.

To ensure plumb holes, I make a jig similar to the one I used to drill out the mortises in the benchtop. It helps guide the bit as you plunge through the benchtop.

Drill the holdfast holes until the lead screw pokes through the underside of the benchtop. Stop drilling. After all the holes are drilled, come back and finish the holes by drilling through the underside of the benchtop. This results in clean holes without a lot of grain ripping out under the benchtop.

INSTALL THE SWING-AWAY SEAT

While your drill is handy, I recommend you install the swing-away seat. Then, after its bolts are in place on the front leg, you can drill the holes in the front leg for holdfasts.

I've had one of these swinging seats on my workbench for a long time – I used to find them at antique malls or through industrial salvage companies (and now Benchcrafted manufactures them). They

THE ANARCHIST'S WORKBENCH

LAY OUT THE HOLES

THE THREE HOLES IN THE FRONT LEG SHOULD BE ON 8" CENTERS FOR A TYPICAL HOLDFAST. AND THEY SHOULD NOT INTERFERE WITH THE BOLTS FOR THE SWINGING SEAT (SHOWN AT RIGHT).

are not just for resting. I sit on mine while I chop out dovetail waste. I do all my drawing and drafting there. I eat my lunch. I answer emails.

I usually install the seat so it's about 17-1/2" off the floor, or about halfway up the leg. This is lower than modern chair height (20"), but it suits my work. Experiment with a stool and some books stacked on its seat to find your ideal height.

After you drill the pilot holes for the seat's bolts, you can drill the 1" holes in the front leg for holdfasts. I like the top hole in the leg to be about 8" from the benchtop. This allows you to clamp a board to the front edge of the benchtop in several positions. The lower two holes are on 8" centers. This allows my holdfasts to store easily without hitting one another. And it gives me three good positions for when I use these holes as a support for a big door or long tabletop clamped in the face vise.

Drill the 1" holes with an auger bit until its lead screw emerges from the back of the leg. I couldn't get an auger bit back there to finish the job, so I used my tapered reamer to finish the job. It did a better job than simply blowing out the back of the leg with the auger.

FLATTEN THE BENCHTOP

Now is the time to flatten the benchtop. It's best to wait until after you've beat it up by adding the planing stop and the holdfast holes, and gooped up the top with epoxy from installing the liners on the jaw.

After 20 years of flattening benchtops, I now take a simpler approach than when I was younger. My approach back then was to treat the benchtop like it was a giant board of wood and flatten it with the guidance of winding sticks and diagonal strokes with my handplanes.

I still use those techniques when I flatten slab benchtops because they are indeed giant boards that twist (two corners high; two corners low) just like a little board.

But a laminated top doesn't twist unless you made a dog's dinner of your glue-ups. Each lamination tends to keep the others in check. So you can use a simpler procedure when flattening a laminated benchtop. I begin with traversing strokes with a jack plane. Then I finish up using with-the-grain strokes with a jointer plane. That's it.

I also don't try to get the benchtop to a level of flatness that rivals a granite plate in a machinist's toolroom. I aim for a benchtop that won't

RIGHT ACROSS
TAKE A STROKE. PULL BACK. SHIFT OVER. TAKE ANOTHER STROKE. PRETEND YOU ARE A MACHINE AND KEEP THINGS REGULAR AND EVENLY SPACED.

ASSEMBLY & VISES

GUMMING UP THE WORKS
THIS IS THE DUST THAT ACCUMULATES AFTER ONE SET OF SHAVINGS. IF ANY MORE GATHERS BACK THERE, THE PLANE WILL STOP CUTTING RELIABLY. CLEAN IT OUT EVERY TIME.

distort my work.

You have a surprising amount of leeway here. Small depressions in a benchtop (say, a few square inches across and a few thousandths of an inch deep) do little to mess up your work. The work lies over the concavities and doesn't bend into them while you plane. Small and large bumps can be a problem. But the jointer plane can mow those down when you flatten the benchtop.

Also important to consider: The most critical surface of the benchtop is the front 8" to 12". The back 40 gets used very little. And when it does get used, you are usually planing up a large panel that will have some inherent stiffness and will have good support at the front of the benchtop to help things stay under control.

In other words, plane the benchtop basically flat and use it. If it gives you trouble (and you absolutely will know when things are bad) then deal with the problem.

THE ANARCHIST'S WORKBENCH

UP & DOWN
When you flatten your benchtop, you'll be glad it's not 36" wide. Work the front part. Then move to the back of the bench and work the rear section of the benchtop. Don't worry about grain direction.

Here's how. Take your jack plane and set it pretty rank. To prevent spelching, bevel off the rear edge of the benchtop with about four or five strokes of the jack. Hold it about 45° to the benchtop. Now take traversing strokes – directly across the benchtop. These should be evenly spaced so that each shaving feathers off into the next one.

Go all the way down the benchtop. Stop.

Take an oily rag and wipe off any dust on the plane's sole. Take your fingernail and clean out the dust collecting between the iron and the back of the mouth. Do this after every round of shavings. Wax the sole with paraffin. Repeat.

Repeat this process over and over until the benchtop is consistent. At the end, it should look like a wave pool – small waves peaking consistently down the benchtop. Check the length of the benchtop with a straightedge (a yardstick will do fine). Make sure there isn't a giant depression or hump along the length of the bench. If there is, fix the problem by working off the high spot(s).

Now switch to a jointer plane. Set your iron fairly rank (yellow pine allows this). Work parallel to the grain. Overlap your strokes. Your arms are likely to be too short to plane all the way to the backside of the benchtop while standing at the front. Go around to the backside to finish the top. Don't worry about a little tear-out on the benchtop. It's a working surface – like a butcher block – not a showpiece.

When all the traversing marks disappear and you are getting full-width, full-length shavings along every part of the benchtop, stop. Check the top with a straightedge and make sure it looks reasonably flat. You will see light under the straightedge (our eyes can see a .001" gap). So don't freak out.

BENCH HOOKS WHERE YOU NEED THEM
Bench hooks are as important as the vise. They should be easy to grab without digging through piles of stuff.

CHAPTER XV
MAKE IT WORK RIGHT

With the vises functioning, many woodworkers add a quick finish (boiled linseed oil) and start building furniture. There is nothing wrong with that approach, except your bench is missing essential gear that makes your work easier. If it were a car you'd be missing the radio, the air conditioning and the ham sandwich.

Building all these accessories takes one full Saturday. And every one of them pulls their weight for decades to come. I recommend you take a deep breath and say, "I'm not done."

BUILD THE SHELF

Many people skip the shelf. I had to nag Megan Fitzpatrick for more than 10 years before she put a shelf under her bench. It took about an hour of labor, and now it's stacked with crap. Victory. *[Editor's note: Now he nags me to clean up the crap under my bench.]*

Because you didn't build a bathroom vanity workbench (yay, you), the shelf is an important storage space. Historically, it is where you put your bench planes when you aren't pushing them. I keep all my appliances down there – shooting boards, Moxon vise, doe's feet, battens, wedges and small bits of wood to protect my work when using holdfasts. There's also lots of room to stack the furniture components I'm working on.

At the end of every project, I clean out the shelf to get rid of the extra or faulty parts that have accumulated down there. Then I start a new project.

I make the shelf using 1-1/4"-thick boards, just like the rest of the components in this bench. For this design there are six 9"-wide boards (cut from 2x10s). And two 2-1/2"-wide boards, cut from crap found sitting on the shelf of my current bench.

As mentioned earlier, you can put a tongue-and-groove joint on the long edges. Or shiplaps. Or nothing. I prefer nothing.

STOP SHIFTING

Put glue on the cleats, then clamp them lightly to the inside of the stretchers. Shift the cleats around so they are flush with the bottom edge of the stretchers. Then apply some real force. Screw them in place with some No. 8 x 3" screws. Remove the clamps.

The shelf boards rest on 1-1/4" x 1-1/4" cleats that are attached to the stretchers with glue and screws.

With the cleats secured, fit the shelf pieces. If your wood is fresh from the lumberyard, don't worry about wood movement – the stuff will shrink as it dries. If your stuff is bone dry and you are in the dry season, leave a 1/16" gap between the shelf boards to accommodate swelling during the humid months.

I cut a small 3/16" x 3/16" bevel on the long edges of the shelf boards for looks. You can merely ease the edges with a block plane or apply a bead with a beading plane.

Then attach the shelf boards to the cleats, two screws in each.

ADD FINISH

Break all the sharp edges with some sandpaper. Now apply a finish – if you wish. Some people don't apply a finish because they don't want to make the wood any slipperier. I can't be this super hardcore because

MAKE IT WORK RIGHT

REVERSIBLE
I'VE NEVER HAD TO REMOVE A SHELF BOARD TO REPAIR IT. BUT IF I HAD TO, IT WOULD BE AN EASY JOB – JUST REMOVE TWO SCREWS.

an unfinished bench looks dirty in short order.

I prefer two different finishes. Sometimes I apply two coats of boiled linseed oil. Just wipe on a thick coat, then use a second rag to remove the excess. Wait for it to dry. Repeat. Linseed oil doesn't protect the wood much, but it's not a slippery film finish or a slick wax and it's easy to renew. Just add more oil.

The other finish I like is a homemade mixture of equal parts boiled linseed oil, paint thinner and spar varnish. The varnish adds a little more protection to the bench against spills. The paint thinner makes the concoction easy to rag on. Application is the same as for the linseed oil.

For this bench I used the oil-varnish blend. We have a ton of it mixed up because we use it all the time.

Don't bother finishing the undersides of the benchtop or shelf. Our ancestors didn't finish those areas either, and their furniture and workbenches survived just fine. If this paragraph makes one of your

DON'T WAX ON
AVOID WAX OR A SLICK FILM FINISH ON YOUR BENCHTOP. THE GRIPPIER IT IS, THE HAPPIER YOU'LL BE. SHOWN IS A MIXTURE OF LINSEED OIL AND VARNISH FROM THE HARDWARE STORE.

eyes twitchy, remember that most over-the-counter finishes cannot block moisture exchange in the wood. So no, your benchtop won't warp.

TOOL RACK

I scoffed at the French tool rack until I built one. The rack is a great place to put chisels, small clamps or other tools (screwdrivers, awls and cutting gauges) while you are working. It's like a tool tray that doesn't accumulate shavings.

The rack is simple to build from wood. The rack is made from a wall that is 5/8" x 3" x 24" and three stand-off blocks that are 5/8" x 3" x 1-1/2". I start with a single board that is 5/8" x 3-1/4" x 30". I crosscut the stand-off blocks from the board then glue them to the wall.

Then rip the glued-up block to 3" wide. Clean it up with handplanes. Glue the rack to the back edge of the benchtop, flush to the benchtop. Then secure it with some heavy nails.

MAKE IT WORK RIGHT

READY FOR WORK
AS SOON AS THE FINISH HAS DRIED, RE-ATTACH THE VISES. YOU ARE READY TO WORK (OR BUILD SOME MORE IMPORTANT ACCESSORIES).

BENCH HOOKS

I can't fathom working without a pair of bench hooks for crosscutting and shooting the ends of small parts. When I first started making bench hooks, I made them from three pieces of wood: the base, the fence and the hook. After seeing traditional old hooks, I stopped that laminating nonsense. There has been quite enough laminating in this book already.

Now my hooks are sawn from one piece of 2x material. You make two rips, two crosscuts and drill two holes. Done. I prefer to make them with a handsaw, for both fun and for practice. Or I cut them on the band saw when I need to make 14 hooks for a class.

The drawing shows the dimensions. I make mine from the scraps of yellow pine left from bench construction. After drilling the 3/8" hole in the ends, I hang them on a nail driven into one of the legs. Do this and in time you will reach for them almost unconsciously, like the turn signal of your car.

READY TO RACK
THE THREE STAND-OFF BLOCKS ARE GLUED TO THE WALL. NOTE THAT THE GRAIN RUNS IN THE SAME DIRECTION ON ALL THE COMPONENTS.

RIGHT PLACE
I'VE EXPERIMENTED WITH PUTTING THE RACK OTHER PLACES. AND SURPRISE, THE RACK WORKS BEST IN THE PLACES THE OLD BOOKS SHOW IT – RIGHT BEHIND THE FACE VISE. DON'T FORGET TO SCRAPE AWAY ANY FINISH YOU APPLIED TO THE BENCH BEFORE GLUING THE RACK ON.

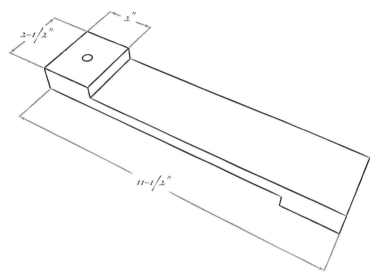

BENCH HOOK DIMENSIONS

DOE'S FOOT

If you have holdfasts, the most important accessory is a couple of doe's feet. This is a notched batten, first brought to my attention by woodworker Richard Maguire. After some research, I found the appliance in Roubo's book with its proper name: doe's foot.

It is a flat piece of wood, maybe 1/2" x 6" x 16". In one end is a V-shaped notch. The notch is made by drawing two intersecting 45° lines. After cutting the notch out, you can call it done. Or you can make it "deluxe animal style" and add some sort of grippy material to the underside. I've experimented with coarse sticky-back sandpaper (#80 grit). And, at the advice of the late Jennie Alexander, adhesive stair tread tape. Both work.

The doe's foot helps restrain work from rotating or spinning on the benchtop. When planing wide boards, press the board against the planing stop. Press the V-notch of the doe's foot against the far corner. Secure the doe's foot with a holdfast. You can then plane the board

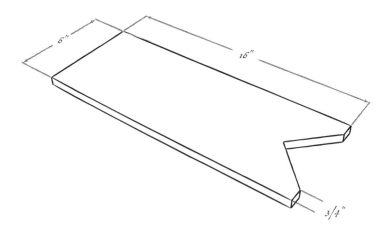

THE DOE'S FOOT IS ESSENTIAL EQUIPMENT

These simple appliances help restrain the rear ends of boards on the benchtop.

MAKE IT WORK RIGHT

across the grain (called traversing), diagonally or with the grain. The doe's foot keeps the board from rotating.

You also can use the doe's foot for holding weird curved stock. Two of them can restrain a curved piece – one doe's foot against the planing stop and one at the rear of the workpiece.

Make a couple and you will find them useful.

BENCH LIGHT

Even when I was in my late 20s, I appreciated a swing-arm architect's lamp at the workbench. It allows you to see knife lines that overhead lights don't illuminate. You can easily rake the light across a board while you are planing to see when the imperfections have disappeared. Plus it helps every operation on a cloudy day.

I always buy vintage architect's lamps. Sad to say they are better than the new lamps you can buy today at office supply stores. You can spend $20 on a no-name (but well-made) vintage example. Or drop $200 on a premium lamp intended for a high-class architect, such as the Luxo brand.

Some people prefer the lamps that also have a magnifying lens. Or ones with two kinds of lights, fluorescent and incandescent. To each her own.

Whatever you do, get a nice LED bulb with a daylight temperature color of 5000K. The LED won't heat up your hands like a slab of roast beef at the cafeteria. The daylight color temperature will help you see the true hue of your finishes and the wood.

Most of the swing-arm lamps come with a flimsy clamp for attaching them to a drafting table. You may throw this away or recycle it. I make a new base for the lamp. It's a block of wood drilled with a hole to accept the shaft of the lamp (usually 1/2"). And there's a dowel sticking out of the block that goes into your holdfast holes. This replacement base lets you move the swing-arm lamp anywhere on the benchtop.

OK, now you are done. You should make some shooting boards and a sticking board for mouldings. But those can wait until the need arises.

ROLL OUT THE BARREL

This is what it's like at the Lost Art Press storefront every day. But without the accordion or bird cage. And without the mess.

CHAPTER XVI
THE 'A' IS NOW AT THE END

When I quit my magazine job, I was done with corporate publishing, but corporate publishing wasn't done with me. My former employer, F+W, still owned the rights to "Workbenches: From Design & Theory to Construction & Use," and it sold thousands of copies, year after year. They had no plans to give it up, and the book was translated into French and German.

Meanwhile, we grew Lost Art Press from a beer-money boondoggle into a small but respectable publishing company. We took the contract I had written while hungover in the Portland, Maine, airport and used it to publish books written by woodworkers we admired. First, I signed Peter Follansbee and Jennie Alexander to write "Make a Joint Stool from a Tree." Then I convinced Matt Bickford to write a book on making mouldings by hand. Joel Moskowitz and I worked together on republishing "The Joiner & Cabinet Maker."

These books sold in ridiculously small numbers at first, but everyone shared in the profits 50/50. In order to continue eating, John, my business partner, kept his day job. And I made money by teaching woodworking classes, selling furniture commissions and (ironically) writing freelance pieces for my old employer.

When "The Anarchist's Tool Chest" came out, however, we sold 1,000 copies in the first few weeks after its release. That's when I knew that Lost Art Press was going to be OK.

We used that same contract with every author (with only technical modifications through the years). Nobody got a better or worse deal. "Treating everyone the same" became our solution to every disagreement we faced.

It worked. About the time we started selling 25,000 books a year, F+W approached me about revising "Workbenches: From Design & Theory to Construction & Use" so it could publish an expanded edition. What I really wanted, however, was to regain the rights to that book, print it in the United States, fix the font size (they had made it smaller) and other changes. But that deal wasn't on the table. So, I revised the text in exchange for – finally – getting paid royalties.

Soon after, F+W began to fail financially. Burdened by debt after multiple acquisitions by venture capital firms, F+W entered bankruptcy protection and opted to sell all its assets at auction, including my book.

John and I decided to attempt to buy the rights to "Workbenches." After years of careful financial planning, cautious expansion and hard work, we had some money we could afford to flush away on lawyers to help us negotiate the deal.

After weeks of working out the details with a team of attorneys, we'd spent enough money on legal fees to buy everyone in my neighborhood a case of beer, but we had a sound, well-reasoned financial offer to buy back the book. It was (in my opinion) overly generous.

It took almost five minutes for them to reject our offer.

Here's the lesson. No matter how successful and hard-working you are, there is always a huge corporation out there that will squash you without noticing. "Workbenches" is now owned by Penguin Random House (PRH), a massive publishing company that's controlled by two even bigger conglomerates (Bertelsmann and Pearson plc).

After a defeat such as this, there is only one thing you can do: Dust yourself off, write a better book and give it away to the world for free.

COMPLETING THE TRILOGY

This book is the third and final installment with the "anarchist" title. The first book, "The Anarchist's Tool Chest," dispelled my fears after quitting my corporate job. Thank you. The second, "The Anarchist's Design Book," allowed me to explore vernacular furniture forms and bring them into a contemporary context. This, I discovered, is a key part of my life's work.

And the third book, "The Anarchist's Workbench," brought me full circle with my woodworking. On the day I picked up a load of yellow pine in 2000 to build my first real workbench, I knew it was the start of something important. And I kept building workbenches (and writing about them) until I arrived at this sentence.

There won't be "The Anarchist's Bird House" book. Or "The Anarchist's Tool Chest 2: Dreams Come True." These three books say what I think is important: Buy good tools, build a simple workbench and build everything in your home.

That goal is not that much different than what my parents were seeking when my family moved to Arkansas in 1973. I still remember it as a bit of shock – both for us and the community around us. Though St. Louis (where I was born) is only 400 miles from Fort Smith, Ark., the food, music, accent, traditions and even the clothing were so different, that it was like emigrating to another country.

A lot of it was for the better. Southern food is the best food. The Ozarks are the prettiest place I've ever lived. The people are, in general, way friendlier. And we had a milkman – a damn milkman – who left us glass jars of milk on our front step.

On the other hand, I attended a segregated school. And the Blue Laws were…well let's just say the manager of the Harp's grocery store will never forget the scene my mother caused one Sunday when they wouldn't sell her a box of tampons.

I was 5 at the time we moved, and I tried to fit in. When I started attending Woods Elementary, I put on a flannel shirt, overalls and cowboy boots (I have destroyed those photos, I assure you).

But I soon realized that fitting in was impossible. We were frauds. Outsiders. I didn't have the accent. And I didn't like guns, hunting or football.

So it was a second shock when my parents bought a farm about 30 minutes south of town. No electricity. No water. We had to build a gravel road to get to it. My father (with our grudging assistance) built two houses at the top of the cliff and made plans to raise goats and strawberries. No power tools at first. Solar shower. Composting toilets. No air conditioning (in Arkansas no less).

And, speaking as a kid, no sugared cereal, no Cokes and no water guns.

We were simply unlike the people around us in Northwest Arkansas. Heck, we weren't like anyone else I met in the middle part of the country. To deal with it, I mostly faked being normal (this worked wonders). As a family we kept our heads down, we did our thing at our farm and we tried to be good neighbors.

We were striving to be homesteaders. But we never used that word.

And that was a good decision. "Homesteading" carries a lot of hippie baggage in Arkansas.

The time has now come for me to stop using the word "anarchist."

To continue to run my life and business the way I always have. Keep my head down. Be good to my neighbors. Be kind to strangers.

For a long time I hoped that being up front about my philosophy and living it by example (such as starting a publishing company based firmly on the principles of mutualism) might make people think: "Huh, maybe anarchism isn't about the violent overthrow of the government and a descent into chaos. Perhaps I should read more about it and give it some thought."

That hasn't happened. When you use words like anarchism, half the population labels you a violent droog, and the other half sniffs that you aren't "pure enough" to use the word.

After 10 years of wearing that word (on my chest, literally, at times), I've decided that I'm tired of labels that divide us.

Whenever we begin a woodworking class at our storefront in Covington, Ky., I like to be on hand to show people where the bathrooms are, to explain the dense urban neighborhood around them and to suggest they avoid political chit-chat during their time here.

"As woodworkers we have a lot more things in common than we have differences," I say. "Try to embrace that for a few days."

I am shocked to tell you this, but the little speech usually works. During the last three years I have watched people from all political persuasions listen to one another, enjoy one another's company and make deep bonds with people they might never associate with (for differences of race, class, politics or geography). I've watched these seemingly odd gaggles of people come back – as a group – to take classes so they could all work together again.

I want to go there.

And if that means I need to stop waving my personal freak flag to help things along, I'm OK with that.

Let me assure you that nothing has changed underneath the hood. I still would rather build things than buy them. And when I do buy something, I try like hell to get it from the women and men who make it, grow it or cook it. I'm suspicious when large governments, corporations and religious institutions intersect. I despise hierarchy. And I'll never have employees. I don't want to control other people's lives, and I don't want my business to grow into something I despise.

But is that anarchism? Cough, cough – nah. I'm just the weirdo who builds stuff at the corner of West Ninth and Willard streets in Cov-

THE 'A' IS NOW AT THE END

ington. You can find me there almost every day, standing at my workbench in the building's barroom. Making furniture until I croak.

Christopher Schwarz
Covington, Kentucky
June 2020

A COPY OF 'LIFE OF THE INFANT,' 1617

Hieronymus Wierix's drawing of a bench was copied far and wide in Europe. It might have helped transmit this workbench form across borders.

APPENDIX A
CONSTANTLY ASKED QUESTIONS

During the last 20 years, I've been asked a lot of questions about workbenches. Most of these questions I've answered 100 times already. That's OK. When people first get focused on building a workbench, they usually haven't read years of blog entries or the five or six books that are available on the topic.

And so they send an email asking what's the best wood to use. Oh, and could I also compare and contrast all the different forms of benches? You know, like, just real quick?

We get these questions almost every week.

Below is a list of the questions I am asked constantly – plus my answers. A lot of this information is covered elsewhere in this book. But this format – question and answer – seems to help some people work through their own doubts.

This chapter also gives me something to cut and paste when replying to emails and letters. Here we go.

QUESTIONS ABOUT WORKBENCH MATERIALS

1. What wood should I use?

There are only a few woods I wouldn't use for a workbench: white pine (too lightweight), expensive exotics (too expensive), rotted wood (too rotted). I recommend you use the heaviest, cheapest and most readily available species in your area. In the South and Midwest, that's yellow pine (the cheapest), followed by poplar and soft maple. Don't worry about the stiffness and other engineering factors. If you overbuild your workbench, it will be plenty stiff and strong.

2. Should the benchtop be a slab? A lamination? Plywood? LVL? Which material works best and survives the long term?

All of these have trade-offs, and all of them work well – both in the short and long term. The choice is less about engineering (all are heavy and stiff enough) and more about aesthetics, economics and the tools you have available. You can make a plywood bench using a table saw and screw gun. A slab bench requires far more (including a forklift). But which looks better? That's your call.

3. What's the best glue for building a workbench?

All the common glues are strong enough – hot hide, liquid hide, PVA, epoxy. Choose one that suits your wallet and the way you work. PVA is cheap and easy to get, and it sets up fast (this can be good or bad). Hot hide glue sets up very fast (again, good or bad). Liquid hide glue might be difficult to purchase in your area and sets up slowly. Epoxy is very expensive, but it fills gaps and can have a slow or fast curing time depending on its formulation. For most woodworkers, PVA (plain old yellow glue) is an excellent choice.

4. Can I use green wood? How green?

Yes. But it's risky. Drier is better. You have no idea how much the components will move as they dry. Benchtops, even thick ones, can twist more than 1" at the corners. If you do receive a fresh slab and need a bench today, build the bench quickly and use stretchers between the legs. The undercarriage and the joinery can help hold the top in place as it dries, reducing its tendency to warp. Also, it's a good idea to orient the top so the heart side of the board faces up.

5. Is it OK to include the pith in my bench components?

I don't recommend it. No matter what your local sawyer might say, a board with the pith included (sometimes called a "boxed heart") will split. The split might be minor, or catastrophic. It depends on the tree. Why risk it?

6. Is air-dried wood better for a bench? Or is kiln-dried OK?

Either is fine. And I can't say that either is better for a bench. Just use the heaviest, cheapest wood that is readily available. For me, the more important question is if the wood is at equilibrium with its environment. If not, let it sit a while. Then build the bench.

7. If I can't find Southern yellow pine in my area, can I use....?

Yes.

CONSTANTLY ASKED QUESTIONS

8. What's the best finish for a benchtop?
Probably no finish is the best. You don't want your benchtop to be slick. You want the work to be easily restrained. If you want to make it look nice, some boiled linseed oil will do that (and give you a little protection from water spills). Or an oil/varnish blend. That will give you even more protection, but it might slicken up the benchtop a bit. Avoid waxes and thick film finishes, unless your workbench is a fashion accessory.

QUESTIONS ABOUT THE FORM OR STRUCTURE
OF A WORKBENCH

9. What style of bench should I build if I use only hand tools?
I think the easiest bench to build with hand tools is an English joiner's bench, sometimes called a Nicholson. If you buy dimensional lumber, there is almost no wood to plane to thickness. It's just cutting boards to length and fastening them together with simple joints, screws or nails. Mike Siemsen's video "The Naked Woodworker" is a good place to explore this.

10. Won't wood movement in the benchtop wreck a Roubo or Nicholson workbench?
I have never seen it happen. The top shrinks and expands, and the base contorts a little. It doesn't affect the working qualities of the bench, and the benches don't pull themselves to pieces.

11. Is it OK to use mixed species of woods when building a workbench?
Sure. There is no issue with strength, longevity or (realistically) differential wood movement. A hardwood top and a white pine base might be an economical way to build a bench. The only real concern is aesthetics. Sometimes a benchtop with strips of walnut and purpleheart through the middle make me throw up in my mouth.

12. What's the best workbench for…
…a beginner?
Probably an English joiner's bench (aka, a paneled bench). It has the fewest joints and is the fastest form to build in my experience. However, any beginner can build a French bench or a fancy German bench. It

just takes a little more time. Don't let your lack of skills snuff out your dreams.

13. ...an apartment dweller?

I would build a small yellow pine bench like the one in this book with nice vises. It would have mass because of the pine and all the features of a full-size bench. Then, when you get a bigger place, you can build a bigger bench and use the same nice hardware. The small bench could go to a friend or become a kitchen island in a Manhattan loft.

14. ...a garage or barn without HVAC?

I would use softwoods, such as yellow pine, fir or hemlock. These woods move less in service than hardwoods. So, if there are wild swings in humidity, you'll see less wood movement.

15. ...a person with very little money?

A bench made with yellow pine or any heavy construction timber. Pound for pound, construction woods are the cheapest and easiest to get.

16. What do you think of a torsion-box benchtop? Or the New-Fangled Workbench? Shaker workbench? How about this other workbench that you've never seen or heard of?

At times, I feel like I'm being baited with this kind of question. You can answer the question for yourself if you think about it for a minute. Your bench needs mass. How easy is it to work on the faces, edges and ends of boards with the bench? Can you modify the bench as your woodworking changes by adding different vises or holdfasts? Does the joinery seem impossibly robust or one step above a slumlord's birdhouse?

17. Should the benchtop be assembled with loose tenons?

This is an ancient way to assemble slabs (made popular by Greek and Roman boat builders). It certainly adds long-term strength. Drawboring these loose tenons can help pull boards together without clamps. If you lack clamps or faith in your glue or edge-jointing skills, this is a good technique to fix those shortcomings.

CONSTANTLY ASKED QUESTIONS

18. Can I glue 8/4 material face-to-face to make a thick benchtop?
Yes. You also can laminate a large quantity of toothpicks to make a benchtop. The trade-off is you need the equipment to do a seamless job. Or you need to be OK with a few gaps. There is a lot of surface area that needs to be glued when you laminate boards face-to-face.

19. Why shouldn't I buy a Lie-Nielsen, Plate 11 or Benchcrafted workbench or a high-end Sjöbergs or Ulmia?
I like building my own workbenches in the same way I like building all the furniture in my house and making pizza from scratch. That doesn't make my furniture or pizza better than store-bought. It's just what I like to do. In fact, I cannot do things any other way because my head is that stupid. If you would rather buy a workbench and spend more time building jungle gyms for owls, do it. As always, *caveat emptor* with tools and woodworking equipment. I've used Benchcrafted, Plate 11 and Lie-Nielsen benches and find them to be great. Sjöbergs are not my favorite. And I haven't tried a recent-vintage Ulmia.

20. Could you evaluate all the workbenches you've encountered in your career and explain to me the best one for my work?
Sure thing. Wait right here.

21. What's your favorite workbench ever?
Probably the one in this book.

22. Which workbenches do you regret building?
None, really. Even the ones that were less successful taught me important lessons. The bench I miss the least is the door on sawhorses.

23. Should I tooth my benchtop like veneer?
Sure. I've tried it. The rough resulting surface seems to help keep your work in place, but that might only be my perception and not an engineering truth. The best reason to do it is that every time someone tooths a benchtop, the internet poops its inter-pants.

24. Is there any case where you would advocate for a tool tray?
Yes, when the tool tray is a box with a lid and three sliding tills. And positioned off to the side of your bench where all your tools are at hand.

25. What's the best way to make my workbench mobile?

Push it. Commercial "mobility kits" don't impress me. I've seen engineered solutions that are more complex than a Jarvik-7 artificial heart. Simple is best. Most benches can be slid across a floor easily. If you want to protect the floor, put a moving blanket under the feet. Honestly, I own workbenches that are almost 400 pounds, and I can move them myself with my scrawny bird-like arms.

26. What's the best height for a workbench?

I think it's somewhere between the historical heights of 28" and 36". Plus, remember that you can endure working in a range of about 3" around your ideal. So, if you can't decide, make the bench a little taller than the internet tells you. Then saw the legs down bit by bit until you find that your work becomes easier. Second piece of advice: Sit down at your bench to do detail work with carving tools, chisels or a router.

27. What's the best way to make my workbench height-adjustable?

This sounds snarky, but it's not. Sit down at a shop stool if you need to be closer to your work. Stand on a stool (or raised platform) if you need to get above it. Adjust your height – not the workbench's.

28. What do you think of these commercial benches that adjust in height?

I don't see a need for them in my workshop. Adjust yourself.

29. What about the casters activated by a foot pedal?

The ones I've tried are not durable enough for a heavy bench.

30. Should my workbench be in the center of the room or against the wall?

Either works, as long as you can move the bench for oddball operations. I shift my bench all the time to do different things. I prefer to have my bench in the middle of the room so I can go around to its backside to take photos. But most people don't need to do that. One caveat: If your bench is lightweight, having it against the wall (or secured to the wall) can make it more stable.

31. If I put my bench near a window, which direction should it face?

The classic shop uses only the beautiful northern light. The real shop will take any window facing any direction.

CONSTANTLY ASKED QUESTIONS

32. Can I drawbore a bench together without glue to make it knockdown?

You can do this once. After you disassemble a drawbored joint, it never goes back together as tightly as it did the first time.

33. How lightweight is too light?

If the bench moves across the floor during normal planing operations, you have a problem. Bolt the bench to the floor (or wall), add weights or build a heavier bench. After experimenting with commercial benches that were on the featherweight side, I've found the typical 60 lb. bench is too light. At about 150 lbs., things begin to work. Above 250 lbs., I don't notice the workbench.

QUESTIONS ABOUT WORKHOLDING

34. Won't the toothed planing stop cut me?

It's unlikely. I've never cut myself after 15 years of daily use. Can it happen? Sure. Have I heard of people getting cut? Only once. Is it mentioned in early texts, which detail many of the possible gruesome injuries in the shop? Not that I recall.

35. I don't want to cut a mortise for the planing stop in my beautiful benchtop. Are there other options?

Sure. You can fasten a moving block to the end of your benchtop. But I think that's lame compared to just chopping a hole in your bench and doing the job right. I totally understand that some people have a mental block about some things: grinding an iron, filing the mouth of a handplane open, doing the Ruler Trick for the first time. The barrier is all in your head. Close your eyes and jump off the tire swing. You'll be glad you did.

36. Do I have to have a face vise? Can't I use just a crochet? Or is that a dumb idea?

Screw-driven vises didn't show up until the 14th century. So yes, you can do excellent work without a screw-driven vise. Yet, the screw-driven vise is enormously convenient. (There's a reason that Record never made a iron crochet – painted blue – for workbenches.) And vises are readily available and inexpensive. (But for the record, I enjoy using a crochet.)

37. What is the best arrangement/placement of holdfast holes?

Three rows. The back row is 3" from the rear edge of the benchtop. The middle row is 10" from the rear edge. The third row is 17" from the rear edge. The holes are 16" away from each other. And the holes are staggered on each row by 8". You might have to adjust these dimensions if you have a very narrow benchtop, but this is the general idea.

38. … of dog holes?

Dog holes should be close to the front edge of your benchtop – usually 2"-3" or so. This allows you to use handplanes that have fences that drop below the benchtop (such as a plow plane). I like to keep my dog holes close together – about 3" on center.

39. What's better: a wooden vise screw or a steel one?

Neither. Both can close quickly and ferociously on your work. Both can last several lifetimes if cared for. Both can be trashed by abuse.

40. What's the best material for lining the jaws of a vise?

I like suede and a cork-and-rubber gasket material (Benchcrafted sells this as Crubber). Avoid cork alone as it's too fragile. Some people like neoprene, but I haven't tried it.

41. What glue should I use to affix the liner for the jaw?

I prefer epoxy. Full stop.

42. Should I install a patternmaker's vise? In the tail vise position? The face vise position?

If you are a patternmaker, yes. And it can go in either position on the bench, according to the historical record. If you are a regular-head furniture maker, this vise has downsides. It's expensive and a trick to install. Most furniture makers don't need one. But dammit, I own one.

43. Why won't my holdfasts cinch down?

Your benchtop might be too thin, so the holdfast cannot wedge itself in place. Or the hole is too big for the shaft, so the holdfast can't wedge in place. Or the hole is not plumb. Or the shaft is too smooth. The least likely reason is the holdfast is poorly made and doesn't have enough spring.

CONSTANTLY ASKED QUESTIONS

44. How flat does my workbench have to be?

The bench has to be flat enough so your work doesn't spring in low spots to the point where you cannot flatten boards with your handplanes. If you work with handplanes, you will know when the benchtop is too wonky because your planes won't do their job. If you don't work with handplanes, flatness is rarely critical.

45. How often should I flatten my workbench?

I flatten a benchtop when I make it. Then I flatten it again when it has become disgusting from glue and abuse. Or when it stops working (as per the previous question). Some people flatten their benchtops yearly. Some do it after every big project. I ain't got time for that. And I haven't found it necessary.

46. What's a vise garter? Do I need one?

Garters are a part of a screw-driven vise that links the screw mechanism to the vise's jaw. With a garter in place, the jaw moves in and out when you move the screw in and out. Without a garter, the jaw moves forward with the screw, but must be pulled back manually when you retract the screw. Do you need one? They're convenient but not necessary.

47. Will I regret not installing a tail vise?

The best path forward is to build a bench that allows you to add a tail vise immediately or in the future. That way you and your work can answer the question (instead of a dumb Kentucky woodworker).

48. Which is better: square dogs or round ones?

Neither. Square dogs don't rotate; round ones do. Your work might need round dogs if it's odd-shaped. Round dogs are easier to install. Both forms are traditional and go back centuries.

49. …steel dogs or wooden ones?

Steel dogs hold better but they will mess up your handplane as soon as you hit one. Wooden dogs don't hold as well, but they don't hurt your handplanes. The choice is yours.

50. What sort of woodwork requires a tail vise?

If you plane up a lot of boards that are similarly sized, a tail vise can be nice. They can also be nice for disassembling a frame that is tightly dry-fit. They are convenient for traversing wide boards with a jack plane or working diagonally with a jointer plane. We have several benches with tail vises or wagon vises. I use a tail vise once every few months.

51. Do I need a board jack (either integral or freestanding)?

These are helpful when you have very long boards (longer than 8') or a face vise that has a poor grip and cannot handle an 8'-long board by itself. They are also handy for edge-jointing long tabletops and mortising doors. If you do big work, they are a godsend. If you don't, they are occasionally useful but are mostly a storage facility for holdfasts.

52. Finally, what wood should I use for my bench?

Oh, do sod off.

TRADITIONAL SHOP IN MINIATURE
This workbench scene, owned by tool collector John Sindelar, shows a complete, functioning shop. But what if you don't own a bench?

APPENDIX B
WORKING WITHOUT A WORKBENCH

There's only one reason that the cheap-o workbench industry exists. And that's because people think they need a workbench to build a workbench (or are truly delusional and think it will be fine for furniture making).

So many woodworkers I've met have spent $200 to $500 on a bench that isn't worth the BTUs to burn. The things wobble like a broken finger. The vises hold like the handshake of a creepy vacuum salesman. They are too lightweight for even mild planing tasks.

You don't need one of these benches to someday construct a "real" bench. In fact, I build benches all the time without the assistance of a workbench. It's easy. Start with sawhorses. Glue up the benchtop on the sawhorses. Sawhorses + benchtop = ersatz bench. Now build the workbench's base on top of that ersatz bench. Put the base and the benchtop together. You're done.

If you want a temporary workbench until you build a "real" workbench, there are ways to get the job done with just a little money and a little frustration. This brief chapter seeks to give you some options.

I know that some of you will insist on buying something as soon as you anoint yourself a woodworker. It's an instinct we're trained into as consumers. Here are a few things to put in your shopping cart instead of a cheap workbench:

• Buy an industrial steel packing table with a hardwood top. You can get these from many, many suppliers (McMaster-Carr is one). These feature a heavy welded steel base and a wooden top that's maple, if you're lucky. These metal tables don't rack like a cheap workbench and cost less (way less if you find a used one). You can screw thin pieces of wood to the top as planing stops so you can plane the faces of boards and legs and the like. And get a large handscrew clamp to stabilize boards when planing them on edge. These packing tables don't come with any vises, of course, but you can fix that with your credit card.

THE ANARCHIST'S WORKBENCH

• Buy a couple bar clamps (you'll need clamps no matter what) that are long enough to span the width of the top of the packing table. Screw a 4x4 below the benchtop right at the front edge of the top – this will allow you to clamp your work to the front edge of the benchtop so you can work on boards' edges and ends.

That's one solution. How about a simpler approach?

• Use your kitchen cabinets, kitchen table or dining table as the workbench. You can clamp planing stops to the tabletop (you'll need a couple F-style clamps for this). Don't forget to buy a large handscrew clamp to help stabilize boards when planing them on edge on the tabletop.
• For working on edges and ends of boards, buy a commercial Moxon vise, which you can clamp to any tabletop or countertop. This vise will let you work on the edges and ends of boards. Even after you build a "real" workbench, you'll continue to use the Moxon and the handscrews.

Is that still too much money? Do you have a public park nearby?

• Use a picnic table. Drive nails or screws into the top to serve as planing stops. With a picnic table you get both high and low working surfaces. You can drive some nails into the picnic table's benches to act as a planing stop and use them like a Roman workbench.
• Buy a couple big handscrew clamps (every woodworker needs these anyway). Clamp or screw these handscrews to the picnic table so they work like vises so you can work on boards' edges or ends.

Here are other time-honored solutions I have observed in the wild.

• Take four pieces of 3/4" x 24" x 96" CDX cheap-o plywood and screw them together face to face to make a 3"-thick benchtop. Screw this benchtop to a used metal desk. The old metal desks that populated schools, warehouses and government offices are ugly, cheap and widely available. They are almost all 30" high. Add a 3"-thick benchtop and you are in the right height range for most Americans. Some of these desks have MDF desktops. Some have sheet metal tops. Either way, you can screw your plywood benchtop to the desk. Bonus: The drawers give you tool storage. Add workholding as above.

• Conscript an old dresser/bureau. This is a three- or four-drawer cabinet for storing clothes. One 19th-century book I read showed how to turn this into a workbench. Attach planing stops to the top of the bureau/dresser. For sawing, keep it simple – use 5-gallon buckets as sawbenches (thanks for that tip, Mike Siemsen). You also could clamp a Moxon vise to the top. The lower drawers are for storing tools. The upper drawer can catch sawdust (not my idea – it was mentioned in the book).

THE APOCALYPSE WORKBENCH

When I teach or demonstrate woodworking on the road, the venue is occasionally luxurious and other times it's more like "Lord of the Flies." I've showed up at woodworking clubs where the workbench on offer was a folding table with metal legs and a particleboard top.

After years of encountering this problem, I learned to travel with an emergency kit of things that allowed me to work without bursting into sweat and tears in front of an audience. Here's the kit:

• Two large handscrews
• Two 36" bar clamps
• Two F-style clamps (usually with 12" bars)
• Thin strips of plywood, usually 3" x 24" and in two thicknesses: 1/4" and 1/2"
• Small clamping pads of scrap plywood, to prevent denting my work when I pinch it
• A few softwood shims
• A couple simple bench hooks for sawing.

This kit has converted many desks and tables into somewhat-functioning workbenches. The handscrews and bar clamps act as face vises. The plywood scraps can be made into planing stops for planing with the grain or across it. And the F-style clamps can clamp my work – or other clamps – to the tabletop.

To be sure, I'm always happy to return home to my workbench. But until I find a way to fit it in an airplane's overhead compartment, this kit has become a way that I can work almost anywhere.

THE ANARCHIST'S WORKBENCH

AN INEXPENSIVE & LIGHTWEIGHT BENCH
This bench weighed 57 lbs. out of the box. Our cats could move it around the shop.

WORKING WITHOUT A WORKBENCH

SAME BENCH AFTER MODIFICATIONS
AFTER ADDING MASS, THE BENCH WEIGHED 130 LBS., AND IT WAS ALMOST USABLE.

THE ANARCHIST'S WORKBENCH

IF YOU BUY (OR INHERIT) A CHEAP WORKBENCH?

Let's say that all your friends warned you against buying a $200 to $300 "hobby" workbench and you went against their advice ("How bad could it be?"). This part of the book is for you. As an experiment, I bought one of these benches for $220 (total with shipping). Out of the box, it weighed just 57 lbs. That's the sort of bench that you want to feed a sandwich.

I decided to see if I could make it into a decent bench for about $50. I came pretty close. Here's what I did.

The bench's base was a lightweight white pine and was assembled with dowels and screws. The two end assemblies were joined with wide pine stretchers. Captured nuts and bolts pulled everything tight, like assembling a bed.

The first thing I did was to glue all the joints in the end assemblies as I put the bench together. The instructions didn't mention glue, but I added it to the dowels and all the mating surfaces. I "sized" the end grain areas with glue and then re-applied glue if the gluing surfaces became dry before clamping the parts together.

Then I bolted the ends together. I added the thin shelf provided by the manufacturer then slapped three layers of scrap construction plywood on top of the thin shelf. This added much-needed mass.

To make the base even more rigid and heavy, I screwed 3/4"-thick plywood panels to the back and ends of the base.

The benchtop was maple and only 1" thick. So I glued and screwed two layers of 3/4"-thick plywood to the underside of the benchtop. The new benchtop thickness of 2-1/2" isn't terrible. I had to drill out the dog holes through the new plywood layers.

The original benchtop was connected to the base with puny screws. I replaced those screws with four sets of 3/8" hex-head bolts, washers and nuts. While I'm not wild about bolting together a bench, it is a step up from using spindly screws.

The workholding on the bench was a skimpy end vise. So I added holes for holdfasts in the benchtop. Then I drilled holes in the front legs so I could put holdfasts or pegs there. I added a crochet to the front edge of the benchtop. Planing edges of boards is now quite easy.

Then I restrained the bench to the floor with lag screws. You can bolt yours to the shop floor or screw cleats to the floor to fence in the

WORKING WITHOUT A WORKBENCH

bench's feet. (While you're down there, check out the bench's feet. They might not sit flat and need to be planed, sawn down or shimmed up.)

With all my modifications, the bench weighed about 130 lbs. – a lot more than when it was born from its shipping box. When restrained to the floor it didn't sway under planing pressure.

It wasn't the worst bench I had ever worked on. (But, to be fair, I have built stuff on folding tables, a rotting porch and a loading dock. The bar is pretty low.)

I don't, however, recommend this path unless you inherit one of these benches. Never ever buy a $220 commercial bench. Not even on a bet. That $220 could buy you more than 900 pounds of yellow pine.

VINTAGE IRON CLAMPS

To squeeze out gaps, invest in about 10 vintage iron clamps. You'll use them for many other tricky glue-ups in the future.

APPENDIX C
HELPFUL TOOLS FOR BENCH BUILDERS

Building a timber-frame workbench isn't like building a birdhouse. I have found there are a few tools outside of the furniture-makers' kit that will help the process. Consider calling this appendix "The Anarchist's Bench-building Addendum to 'The Anarchist's Tool Chest.'"

Snappy title, that.

HEAVY METAL CLAMPS

I mentioned this in the chapter on building the benchtop, but it bears repeating. A laminated benchtop will laugh at your lightweight aluminum and nylon clamps. If you want tight joints and you don't want to glue up your benchtop one board at time, you need heavy iron or steel clamps.

As far as I know, these aren't available new. So you need to buy vintage. The good news is they are readily available and are usually pretty inexpensive when you buy them in person (shipping online can be a killer).

The best clamps have these features:

• A movable pad with a spring-loaded tooth that bites into notches in the clamp's bar. The clamp head will not slip under pressure, unlike clamps that use a friction clutch.

• A heavy Acme-thread screw. My clamps have a 5/8"-diameter screw with square threads. The clamps with the little triangle-shaped teeth are puny and worthless.

• A handle that is an offset crank. A straight handle will not let you unlock the full force of the clamp. A cranked handle will.

IMPORTANT FEATURES OF IRON CLAMPS
The Acme-thread screw and crank handle allow you to apply punishing pressure. The notched bar ensures the sliding head won't move under that pressure.

There are many brands of vintage clamps that have these same features in a slightly different configuration. Instead of a spring-loaded tooth, the clamp might have a removable pin. Instead of an L-shaped cranked handle, it might have a handle that is hinged so you can rotate it 90°. The screw might be 1/2" or 3/4" in diameter. Or metric.

Bottom line: If the clamp won't allow the pad to ever slip, if the thread is Acme and robust, and if the handle allows you to add force at 90° to the screw, buy the clamp. We have a dozen of them in the shop, and I wish we had a dozen more.

HELPFUL TOOLS FOR BENCH BUILDERS

TAPERED REAMER
Designed for making joints in Windsor and stick chairs, the tapered reamer is helpful for easing the drawbored holes in your tenons.

TAPERED REAMER

For years I used drawbore pins to deform the hole through the tenon. The deformation allows the oak peg to bend (instead of explode) when it hits the tenon. Another option is to use a tapered reamer on the hole to create the same effect. You just ream the hole that passes through the tenon a little. Too much reaming, however, will weaken the tenon.

There are lots of vintage reamers out there, especially in the plumbing trade. Or you can buy one made for chairmaking.

Here's how I use it. First I trace the shape of the hole through the leg (or benchtop) onto the tenon. Mark the offset and drill the hole through the tenon. Then ream the hole. There is no need to ream beyond the boundary you traced on the tenon. Ream the exit hole on the tenon a little, too. This method, I have found, lets me use a strong offset (1/8" or 3/16") with no failures.

BARR CHISEL
WHEN CLEANING UP THE MORTISES IN THIS BENCH, A WIDE CHISEL IS HELPFUL. IF YOU WANT THE BEST, BUY A BARR.

2" HEAVY CHISEL

Your 3/4" bevel-edge chisel is not going to like bashing out the mortises in the benchtop and the legs. A heavy 2" chisel will make the job a joy. And you will love having that wide chisel for furniture work – especially defining tenon shoulders and removing waste material for bevels.

I rarely recommend brands, especially in a book. But the bench chisels from Barr Specialty Tools in McCall, Idaho, are the best I have found. Barr Quarton hand-forges each one. The 2" bench chisel shown above takes and holds an incredible edge.

For years I have used vintage wide chisels because new ones weren't available from good manufacturers (such as Lie-Nielsen Toolworks) or they just plain sucked. But even the vintage ones were of spotty quality and didn't hold an edge as well as I wanted.

HELPFUL TOOLS FOR BENCH BUILDERS

WOODOWL AUGER BITS
THESE BITS ARE SHARP, CUT QUICKLY AND RARELY CLOG.

WOODOWL AUGER BITS

Again, I dislike recommending brands. But again, here is an exception. WoodOwl auger bits are the best for bench building. They plow through thick and heavy stock without complaint. So they are ideal for boring holes for mortises freehand (don't use them in a drill press) and drilling holdfast holes. The only downside is they are metric, so the U.S. Customary Units marked on the package are an approximation.

Look for the WoodOwls labeled "tri cut" or "ultra smooth." Those are the ones that work best for bench building.

BENCH SCREWS
Iron

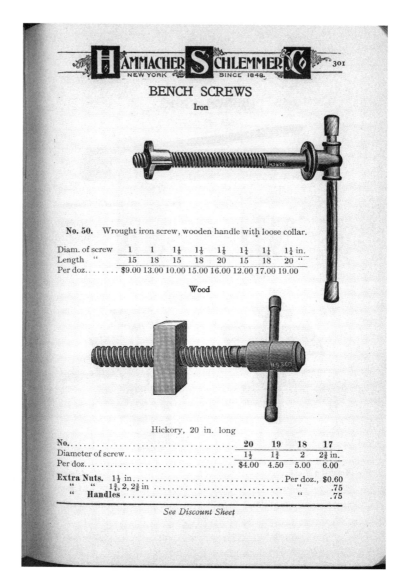

No. 50. Wrought iron screw, wooden handle with loose collar.

Diam. of screw	1	1	1⅛	1⅛	1⅛	1¼	1¼	1¼ in.
Length "	15	18	15	18	20	15	18	20 "
Per doz.......	$9.00	13.00	10.00	15.00	16.00	12.00	17.00	19.00

Wood

Hickory, 20 in. long

No.	20	19	18	17
Diameter of screw	1½	1¾	2	2⅜ in.
Per doz.	$4.00	4.50	5.00	6.00

Extra Nuts. 1½ in. .... Per doz., $0.60
    "   " 1¾, 2, 2⅜ in .... " .75
    " **Handles** .... " .75

See Discount Sheet

HAMMACHER SCHLEMMER CATALOG
BY THE 19TH CENTURY AND THE ADVENT OF COMMERCIAL BENCHES, WOODWORKERS HAD ALREADY FIGURED OUT THE IDEAL FORMS AND VISES.

APPENDIX D
A WORKBENCH TIMELINE

This historical record of workbenches begins (for now) with the eruption of Mount Vesuvius in 79 A.D. Then for about 1,700 years, woodworkers refined the workbench in fits and starts, with most major innovations occurring before 1812.

The following timeline is based on images and extant workbenches in Western countries. While similar and interesting timelines could be developed for Asia, Africa and the New World, this timeline is concerned with Europe.

This abbreviated timeline was generated after years of research by Suzanne Ellison and me. For each entry, we have listed the approximate date, the style of the bench shown and the bench's workholding. The first time a feature appears in our timeline (not necessarily in the wild) it is listed in *italics*.

I don't have a good handle on when the crochet (or hook) first appeared on workbenches. I suspect it is well before 1565, which is when it appears in the following timeline.

The more research we do, the more we know that this timeline is – at best – imprecise. And we hope that future generations will improve upon it.

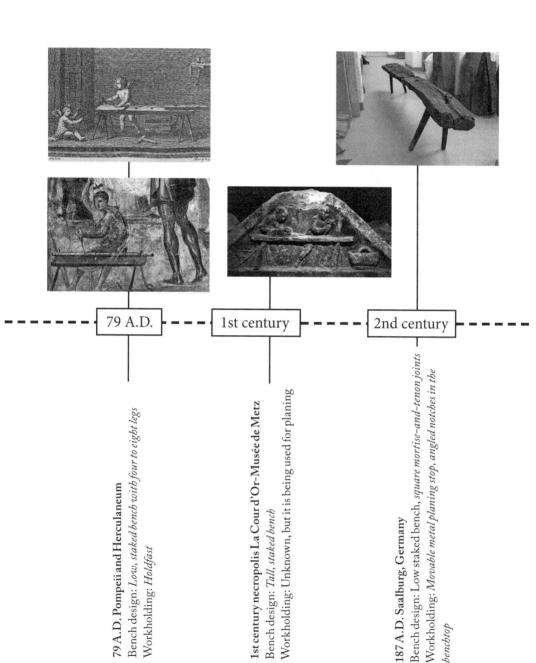

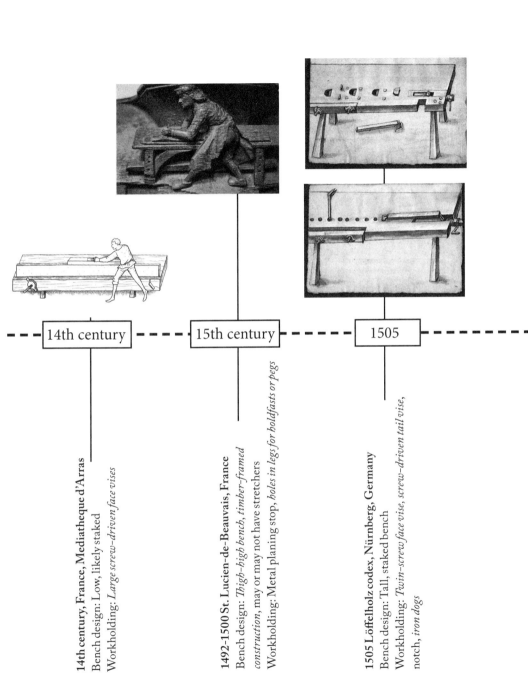

14th century

14th century, France, Mediatheque d'Arras
Bench design: Low, likely staked
Workholding: *Large screw-driven face vises*

15th century

1492-1500 St. Lucien-de-Beauvais, France
Bench design: *Thigh-high bench, timber-framed construction, may or may not have stretchers*
Workholding: Metal planing stop, *holes in legs for holdfasts or pegs*

1505

1505 Löffelholz codex, Nürnberg, Germany
Bench design: Tall, staked bench
Workholding: *Twin-screw face vise, screw-driven tail vise, notch, iron dogs*

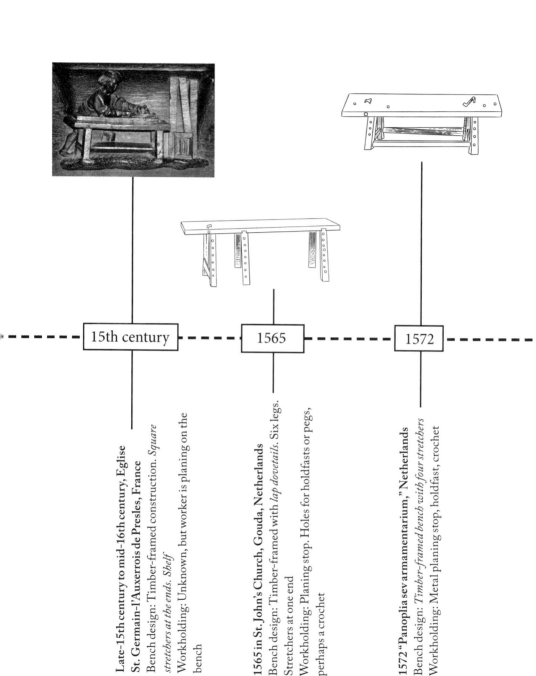

| 15th century | 1565 | 1572 |

Late-15th century to mid-16th century, Eglise St. Germain-l'Auxerrois de Presles, France
Bench design: Timber-framed construction. *Square stretchers at the ends. Shelf*
Workholding: Unknown, but worker is planing on the bench

1565 in St. John's Church, Gouda, Netherlands
Bench design: Timber-framed with *lap dovetails*. Six legs. Stretchers at one end
Workholding: Planing stop. Holes for holdfasts or pegs, perhaps a crochet

1572 "Panoplia sev armamentarium," Netherlands
Bench design: *Timber-framed bench with four stretchers*
Workholding: Metal planing stop, holdfast, crochet

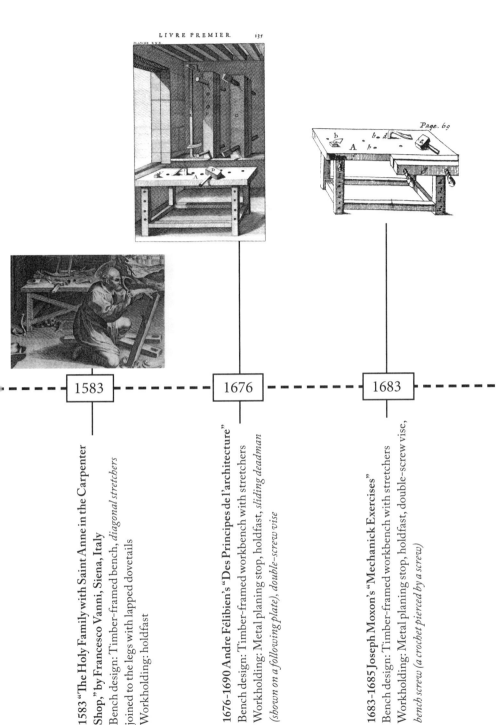

1583 "The Holy Family with Saint Anne in the Carpenter Shop," by Francesco Vanni, Siena, Italy
Bench design: Timber-framed bench, *diagonal stretchers* joined to the legs with lapped dovetails
Workholding: holdfast

1676-1690 Andre Félibien's "Des Principes de l'architecture"
Bench design: Timber-framed workbench with stretchers
Workholding: Metal planing stop, holdfast, *sliding deadman (shown on a following plate), double-screw vise*

1683-1685 Joseph Moxon's "Mechanick Exercises"
Bench design: Timber-framed workbench with stretchers
Workholding: Metal planing stop, holdfast, double-screw vise, *bench screw (a crochet pierced by a screw)*

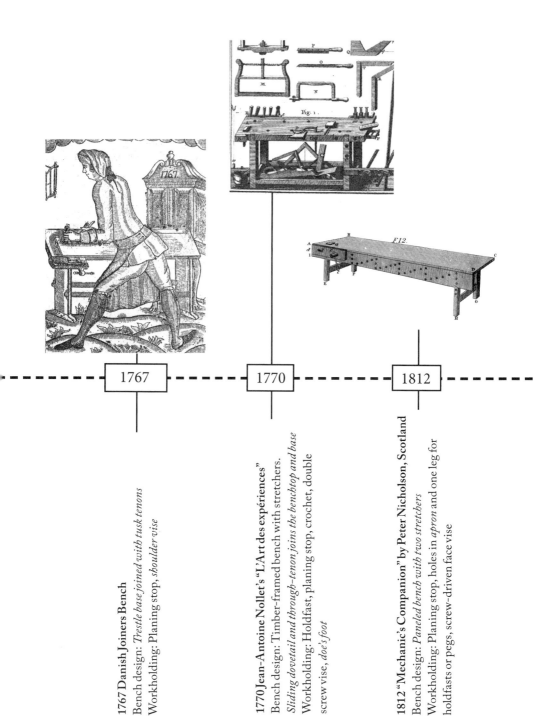

1767 Danish Joiners Bench
Bench design: *Trestle base joined with tusk tenons*
Workholding: Planing stop, *shoulder vise*

1770 Jean-Antoine Nollet's "L'Art des expériences"
Bench design: Timber-framed bench with stretchers. *Sliding dovetail and through-tenon joins the benchtop and base*
Workholding: Holdfast, planing stop, crochet, double screw vise, *doe's foot*

1812 "Mechanic's Companion" by Peter Nicholson, Scotland
Bench design: *Paneled bench with two stretchers*
Workholding: Planing stop, holes in *apron* and one leg for holdfasts or pegs, screw-driven face vise

ACKNOWLEDGMENTS

The following people and organization played large roles in the development of this book:

Narayan Nayar: For goosing me in the right direction (without killing the goose)

John Hoffman: For agreeing (immediately) to my plan to make this book free

Megan Fitzpatrick: Who edited every draft chapter of this book, even the crappy ones I threw away in the end

Suzanne Ellison: My partner in a never-ending search for old workbenches

Kara Gebhart Uhl: For finding many embarrassing errors

Lucy May: For never complaining about me working, even at 2 a.m.

Phil Nanzetta: Our ever-patient print broker, who bends over backward so we can experiment with different manufacturing techniques

The now-defunct F+W Media: The people of this once-great company gave me the best job I ever had. They showed me how to make quality books with little overhead. And I likely would still be there if it weren't for the greed of a few vulture capitalists.

COLOPHON

"The Anarchist's Workbench" is set in Adobe Caslon Pro, 10.5 point over 12-point leading. Chapter headings are in 12 point and subheadings are in 9-point type. The book is printed on #70 matte coated paper. The signatures are Smyth-sewn. The book is casebound with a square back and 98-point boards. The cloth cover is from Pearl Linen. The book was printed by Signature Book Printing in Gaithersburg, Md., on a web press.